MW01602008

3/1999

Look Homeward

Look Homeward

By James M. Boyte, Sr.

O   R   C   P   R   E   S   S

7721

Haven Reformed Church Library
5350 North 25th Street
Kalamazoo, Michigan 49004

Copyright © 1996 by James M. Boyte, Sr.
Library of Congress Cataloging
in Publication Data:
Boyte, James M., Sr.
Look Homeward

95-068899
ISBN 1-882270-35-5

No part of this book may be reproduced
or utilized in any form or by any means.
Published in the United States of America
by ORC Press.
Inquiries should be addressed to:
Editor: ORC Press
1495 Alpharetta Highway, Suite I
Alpharetta, Georgia 30201

*Dedicated to my wife and children and
to the memory
of my mother and father.*

Contents

———◆———

Foreword

Look Homeward is a true story of joy found in the midst of loneliness. On top of a mountain in Turkey, not far from the Soviet Union in the area where Caesar once stood and made his famous statement, "I came, I saw, I conquered," a small number of American soldiers seek to bring their loneliness to God. Desiring to return to the warmth of home, many months of loneliness for these soldiers slowly turns to joy as they undertake the long struggle, in a Moslem country, of financing and building one of the most beautiful chapels ever built. Eventually, a permanent military installation is built that will serve for years to come as a listening post on the Soviet Union. Through alterations of the plans for the installation, what was to be a temporary chapel becomes the first permanent building. The comfort and joy of a dog and two small children help to strengthen the soldiers as they live from one day to the next. Through reading *Look Homeward*, the reader will be able to experience something of the true joy that can come in the midst of loneliness.

Chapter 1

—◆—

I was sitting at my desk, talking with a student when the phone rang. "Is this Dr. Boyte?"

"Yes, it is," I answered.

"The James Boyte who helped build the chapel in Turkey?"

"Yes, that's correct," I replied quite anxiously.

"I'm Chaplain Whaylon from Fort Bragg. It's taken some time to locate you. The reason I'm calling is to let you know that our chaplain in Turkey has been trying to reach you. He wanted to tell you that since the fall of the Soviet Union, our military base at Sinop is being phased out and as of next week, the base will be turned over to the Turkish government. We thought it was important to let you know that through negotiations with the Turkish officials the chapel at Sinop will continue as a place of worship." The chaplain paused.

I didn't say anything. I was thinking.

"Are you still there?"

"Yes, I'm still with you."

"Do you have any questions?"

—◆—

"I don't think so. It's just that I always planned to go back. There is so much that happened."

The chaplain talked a little more and then we hung up. I sat back in my chair. There was so much to think about. The fall of communism—it seemed to have happened overnight, defying the minds of all human beings. As we were building the chapel, the Governor of the Sinop Province told me that maybe with the chapel facing across the Black Sea toward Russia it would help our friends across the pond. Now that the war against communism is finally over, I thought, maybe he was right, maybe God had intervened. Then I thought back through the many struggles and pictured in my mind the inscription that was housed in the vestibule of the chapel. In conclusion it read:

> *After almost two years of building, the first religious services were held in the chapel on Christmas Eve 1958. This house of God stands as a symbol of the zeal and dedication of the men who gave their time and ability to the glory and honor of God and our country.*

Throughout the day I continued to think about the chapel, it was so long ago and yet so much a part of my life. The day's work was completed and I was driving home. I looked at my watch as I drove in, it had taken almost an hour. I picked up my briefcase and started in. There was no one home. Jan and the children must have gone somewhere. I heard one of the cows lowing. I sat the briefcase down and walked across the field down to where the old log house had stood.

It seemed like only yesterday as I recalled Dad standing near the edge of the field, watching him with the yard hens and the little chicks. The night before my twin brother, John, sister Sylvia, and I all finished high school together. A year earlier I watched Mom crying as my older brother, Joe, joined the army and was leaving for Okinawa.

I knew as I got closer to Dad, seeing him gazing across the field, he was saddened by the thought that soon we'd all probably be leaving home. We'd been a close family; I suppose a closeness that was magnified because we never knew how much longer Dad would be with us. Several years earlier he'd been hurt in a truck accident, leaving him unable to work. As a family, we worked with others on their farms, pooling our money to buy food.

"All the baby chicks there, Dad?" I asked as I walked up behind him.

"Still all here," he answered, knowing that the hawks had been trying but so far without any luck. "Just looking at the weeds in the field," Dad said.

"If old Club Foot hadn't died, Dad, I would've got the field plowed and we would've had it planted."

At a distance there was the familiar sound of a tractor running. "Jim Boy," Dad said, as he turned facing me, "someday we'll get a tractor and do the farming we've always talked about."

"Yeah, Dad, and one of these days we'll have broilers in the old chicken house again."

"I hope so," Dad said as he turned looking toward the empty chicken house.

"Come on, it's time for supper," Mom called.

A little later John and I were lying awake in bed. We'd always slept together, helping to keep each other warm during the winter. I was looking up at the log rafters. Because of Dad's accident we'd been unable to pay for our house and for a period of time we'd moved into one room of my uncle's house, and then using old Club Foot to snake logs out of the woods, we'd built our log house.

"You're leaving, aren't you?" John asked, recognizing my restlessness.

"Yeah," I answered, feeling a closeness that was ours since birth.

John and I talked on, recalling many of the cherished

times in growing up. Some not as cherished as others. There was the time I'd failed the first grade and even though John passed, the decision was made by our teacher and Mom to hold John back. Whether the decision was right or not, for the last twelve years, Sylvia, John and I worked together, played together, and studied together.

It was getting late, John and I stopped talking. Soon I could hear a little snore; I knew he was asleep. I turned and looked at my rifle placed in the corner of the room. It brought back memories. Following Dad's accident, as small children our Christmases continued with anxiousness. Prior to the accident there were more toys, then it became mostly goodies consisting of fruit, dried raisins, and some candy. While there was little money for toys, there was always a little something placed under the Christmas tree. Sometimes it was little dolls for Sylvia made by Mom and then there were wooden toys made by Dad for the boys. As we got a little older, Mom and Dad were determined that we have a little more than goodies. We were in the seventh grade and it wouldn't be long until Christmas. Like always before we knew there would be something. As I continued looking at my rifle I recalled getting up early on that Christmas morning. Placed under the Christmas tree with my name on it was the rifle that belonged to Dad. I turned my head and looked at the night stand where John had placed some of his belongings. I could hear the ticking of his watch, the one that belonged to Dad, given to him the same Christmas.

A couple of days passed. Mom and I were talking. "What's wrong, Son?" she asked.

"Mom, I'm leaving. I know how much Dad wants us to farm, but old Club Foot has died and we don't have a tractor. There's no way we can farm now."

"Are you going back to the oil fields?" Mom asked, knowing I'd spent the previous summer roughnecking in Pecos, Texas.

"Not this time, Mom. I'm going to Washington State

with Jerry and his family. Jerry has been telling me that when he graduated he and his family were moving to Washington State. They've invited me to go along."

I watched as Mom tried not to let her emotions show. Facing me, I saw some tears as she spoke. "Wish I'd known earlier, it'd given me some time to get your clothes ready."

"Don't worry about that, Mom. I've already checked, I've got enough clothes."

"But you've got some in the dirty clothes. I saw them today," Mom said, moving about more rapidly.

"Mom, just reassure Dad that I'll be coming back. I'll be sending you some money for food. If there's any extra, have Dad save it for the farm."

"We'll be okay, Son. Just write us often, that'll mean so much."

Jerry and his family drove out to get me. I said good-by to John and Sylvia, and then I reached and hugged Mom and then I hugged Dad. I knew as the car was leaving and I took one last look, it wouldn't be the same anymore.

It took four days to make the trip to Republic, Washington. Using most of the money that Mom insisted I take, I rented a room for one week.

I was anxious to get work. It was late in the afternoon when we arrived. The next morning I was up early. Jerry told me if I would go out walking and begin to ask around I shouldn't have any trouble finding work. It was much different from the oil fields where for miles and miles there was nothing but flatness, only the pumping of oil and oil rigs to be seen. As I walked along, hearing the roaring engine of a truck loaded with logs, it was very evident that I was in logging country. I stopped in a restaurant just to look and maybe have a chance to talk with someone. One of the men sitting at a table heard the door open. He stopped eating just long enough to glance at me. I could see that these were big men used to rough, rugged work. I had done some hard work, too, but I was a small fellow. I only weighed 143 pounds.

I stopped walking and was standing when the waitress spoke. "Would you like something to eat?" she asked.

"No, Ma'am. Maybe a cup of coffee."

"Where are you from?" one of the men asked in a gruff unfriendly voice.

"I'm from North Carolina."

"A boy like you; you're a long way from home aren't you?"

"Yes, Sir. I finished high school and came out here with a friend."

I didn't say anything else. I knew I was a stranger. I waited until the men were gone. Then there was only the waitress and me.

"You say you're from North Carolina?" she asked.

"Yeah, I came out with a buddy of mine. Back home there's not much work. I thought I might find something out here."

"You stay around here long and work these hills, you'll grow up."

"Any work around that you know of?"

At first the waitress didn't answer. I began to think she was ignoring me. "You got a car?" she finally asked.

"No, but I can walk if you know where I might get some work."

"The old man that owns a mill about three miles down the road was in here the other day. He said something about needing to hire some workers. You might try there."

"Thanks," I said as I handed the waitress enough money to pay for the coffee. I started down the road. Once in a while the dust rolled up from a truck passing by. Finally I was there. On the back side of the mill was water, a lake that was used for transporting logs. Feeling a little nervous, I walked up to the gentleman in the office and asked for a job.

"Son," he said, "do you think you're man enough?"

"I don't know, Sir. I realize I'm young, but I've done a lot of work in my life."

"You aren't very big."

"I realize that too, Sir, but you see I'm a long way from home. I've come all the way from North Carolina."

"Okay. We'll give it a try. You've got a week. By the way, what's your name?"

"Jim. Jim Boyte."

"Bill's my name and this is George. You'll be working with him."

"Thanks," I said. "Thanks for giving me a try. I'll work hard." I wasn't concerned about what kind of work I would be doing. I was happy. I had just got a job.

"I hope you can swim," George said as we walked behind the mill. "You see those logs," he said pointing to the logs in the water. "That's where you'll be working."

My job was guiding logs in the water, directing them to a conveyor that transported them into the mill. The week passed and the job was mine.

I became a frequent visitor at the restaurant. My favorite waitress, Dana, the one I first met, seemed to take a special interest in me; like she accepted me as one of the men. One evening I stopped by to see her.

"George came in today. We were talking about you," she said.

"About me? What did George have to say?"

"You know George. He doesn't say much. I was just talking with him."

"But what did he have to say?"

"I asked him how you were doing. He said you were a good worker. Said you were learning how to stay on the logs more than in the water."

"That George. He'd never tell me he likes my work. Guess he thinks I would ask for a pay raise."

"You're laughing," Dana said.

"That water. George was right. You should have seen me. Just a good thing it's not winter."

"Like I told you before. You stay around long enough, you'll become one of the men."

"Maybe so," I answered knowing I was already having thoughts of leaving. Earlier in the day I received a letter from Mom. She didn't have to say it in the letter, but I knew how much they would like for me to be home. John got work in a clothing store and Sylvia was looking for work. Just wish my job paid more, I thought. That way I could save some money and be able to send more to Mom and Dad.

It was two weeks later when I stopped by the restaurant to let Dana know I was leaving.

"Give it more time," she said. "You've only been here for the summer."

"I know but it's time for me to move on."

"You going back home?"

"Not now. The other day I was talking with George. He told me about being in the merchant marines when he was younger. About how he'd been able to travel and save some money."

"So you're thinking about joining the merchant marines, are you?"

"Yeah. That way I'll be able to travel and make enough money to go back home and farm someday with Dad."

"When you leaving?" Dana asked.

"In a few days," I replied.

"You know, you remind me of that song playing on the jukebox."

"What do you mean?"

"You're like the Wayward Wind, always on the move," Dana replied.

A couple of days later I stood beside the highway hitch-hiking. I was going to Seattle. George told me it was a couple hundred miles. No one was stopping. I began to think maybe I should have bought a bus ticket. But the money, I wanted to send it to Mom and Dad. More than two hours passed and I was still standing. The Wayward Wind, I began to think, maybe Dana was right.

It took most of the day and all night. Finally the next morning I was there walking through the streets of Seattle. Everything was so different, nothing like I'd ever seen before. Horns honking, cars bumper to bumper, the rapid movement of people walking. Everything so busy. So many people but no one to talk to. I kept walking, hoping I was going in the right direction.

Thanks to one gentleman, finally I arrived at the Merchant Marine Office. After traveling all night, I wasn't very presentable. I tried to tidy up before going in.

"Can I help you?" the gentleman asked as I walked in.

"Yes Sir, I'd like to join the Merchant Marines."

"How old are you?"

"I'm nineteen and a half," I replied, turning my hands hoping he would see the roughness of them.

"Nineteen and a half," he replied with a broad smile. "You're too young. You've got to be twenty-one."

I dropped my head and walked out. I didn't know what to do. I started walking. Three hours later I was still walking. Finally I sat down and watched the people passing by. I was getting hungry. I could smell the food in a restaurant. I pulled out my wallet; only thirty dollars left, the rest I had sent home.

"You got a dollar?" an old man asked as he walked up to me.

I looked at him. He was feeble. I knew he couldn't work. "Here is fifty cents," I said. Then I got up and started walking again. For the moment my dreams of the future seemed to have disappeared. I didn't want to be a beggar like so many I was seeing. Finally I walked into an old store.

"Would you like to buy something?" the man asked.

"No, Sir. I'm just looking. There was a lot of canned food. It all looked good. Finally I reached down and picked up a can of beans. Not too expensive, I thought as I walked over to pay him. As I started out the door looking toward a passing car, I slightly bumped into a lady.

Before I could say anything, she said in an angry voice, "Young man!" and then she stopped talking as if she didn't know what to say.

"I'm sorry, Ma'am. I shouldn't have been looking the other way." She must have seen the can of beans in my hand. Maybe that's why she stopped talking.

Stopping next to an old building, I pulled out my knife and opened the beans. It's so different from home, I thought as I kept watching the people go by.

I finished the beans and started walking down the road. I was having thoughts of Mom and Dad. Over the hills and valleys lies home, the place I'm sure that will always be home. The road that brought me out here slowly winds its way back, I thought.

Several hours later I was still walking, trying to get outside of Seattle. Stopping by a service station I washed up and changed clothes. There was no reason to walk any further. It was late in the evening and I was 3300 miles from home. I began to hold up the sign I made, BOUND FOR NORTH CAROLINA, hoping someone would pull over.

Time continued to pass. The cars and trucks rushed by. Patience, I thought, someone will pick me up. A few minutes later, on down the road, I saw a car pull over. I picked up my little bag and quickly moved down the road. As I opened the door the gentleman spoke.

"Howdy," he said.

"Howdy. Thanks for stopping. It's been a long day."

"So you're on your way to North Carolina?"

"Yes, Sir. That's my home. I came out here when school was out. I first landed a job in Republic. It wasn't paying much so I decided to move on. I thought I'd try the merchant marines. That's why I came to Seattle. It didn't work; I was too young. Now I'm going back home."

"I'll take you about a hundred miles. That'll help you a little."

"Yes, Sir. It sure will."

"When I was young I traveled a lot, had a lot of jobs but never seemed to get anywhere. I guess that's the way life is."

"Yeah," I answered as I watched the movement of life along the road; an old man leading a horse with a child on its back, a father playing ball with his son. People having a good time, maybe that's what life is all about.

Coming to a stop the gentleman spoke, "Take care," he said as I got out.

"Thanks. Thanks a lot."

. . . .

Several persons had stopped for me, and the distance home wasn't much further. It hadn't been a bad trip. I'd got to meet some mighty fine people.

Standing along the road in Tennessee, the thoughts of home became dearer as each car passed. My clothes weren't too clean. I hadn't taken time to wash what few I had for several days. Maybe that was why no one was stopping to pick me up. I was getting hungry. What little money I had was gone. Standing for awhile and sitting for awhile, I thought about my life. I moved a finger and watched it. Then I moved a foot and watched it. I spoke some words and listened to them. How great, I thought, life, my life, I must not take it for granted. Apparently I was meditating and not putting forth much of an effort to catch a ride when a car pulled over. I picked up my bag and was getting in when the old man spoke.

"Howdy," he said. "I wasn't sure if you were hitchhiking."

"Yes, Sir. I'm kinda tired. I've been on the road a week. I'd been sitting back there several hours and for the last little while I suppose I'd been thinking more than hitchhiking. It isn't much further to my home. I'm from North Carolina."

"That's where I'm going," he said. "You look hungry. Let's stop and eat."

"Sir, while you eat I'll clean up in the restroom. I need to wash up. I'm not really hungry, and besides when I get home Mama will have something for me. I'll just get a drink of water."

"Okay," he said.

The meal was over and we continued on. Later, I was getting out of the car. "Thanks a lot," I said. A couple more rides and I was just about home. Finally in the night I arrived in Carthage. Mom and Dad didn't have a phone, and besides I didn't have any money for a pay phone. It was just a few miles. I could walk the rest of the way. Dogs barked along the way and I knew that in times past I'd been frightened. I was walking on down the road almost too tired to be very excited. The moon was shining. Our house, I could see the metal roof on our house. I knew it wouldn't be long before daybreak. I heard a rooster crow. It's surely different from the big cities, I thought.

I knocked on the door. Not wanting to scare anyone, I called, "Dad, it's me, Jim. I'm home." I knocked again. "Dad, it's me, Jim."

"That you, Jim Boy" Dad asked excitedly.

"Yeah, it's me. I'm home."

In an excited voice, "Good boy," Dad said. "Just a minute, I'll open the door."

Soon Mom, Dad, John, and Sylvia were all up. "It's sure good for you to be home, Son," Dad said. "Have you come back to stay?"

"I'm not sure. There's not much work around here. I suppose I could get a job in a mill but I don't want that. How have things been here?"

"About as usual," John answered. "I got a job at Jones' clothing store. Sure been lonesome though with you not here. There hasn't been much to do."

"Jim, you look tired," Mom said.

"A little, Mom. I've been on the road a little over a week."

"We kept going to the mail box hoping to hear from you, Son. Your dad kept saying maybe we'll get a letter tomorrow."

"I wrote a couple times, Mom, but I meant to write more often. I was constantly thinking of you all. I don't know why, I've just never been much at writing. "

. . . .

With the passing of the next several days, I was becoming more restless. I wanted to farm but there was no opportunity. Dad often seemed hurt as he watched my restlessness. Dad and I were standing next to the old chicken house looking across the field.

"Son, you remember when we moved here? You worked so hard to get the fields cleared."

"Our dream will still come true, Dad," I replied, recalling his happiness as he watched the clearing of the land.

"You hear that? It sounds like old times," Dad said calling my attention to the sound of a crow flying overhead.

I knew what Dad was talking about. Back when we planted the fields, the crows would fly in and pick up the seeds.

Listening to the call of the crow, there was nothing to worry about now as I watched him fly on out of sight in search of another field. "We'll feed those crows again someday, Daddy," I said, observing that he was having difficulty walking.

"It must be the mail," Dad said, anxiously looking toward the road as we could hear a vehicle coming in. I knew it was Dad's hope there'd be a letter from Joe.

It was the mailman. I'll check the box, Dad," I said, knowing he couldn't walk very fast. I opened the mailbox. "We got a letter from Joe," I anxiously called to Dad.

"Read it," Dad said.

Opening the letter I started reading.

Dear Mom, Dad, John, and Sylvia,

    Just ten more months and I'll be home. I just can't wait; I'm so anxious to see you all.

    Have you heard from Jim yet? I often times think about him and wonder what he is doing. I'm sure it's quite different now—the school bus not stopping anymore, me and Jim gone, wondering what John and Sylvia will be doing in the future...

I finished the letter and took it to Mom. The importance of a letter to them was clearly visible as they all huddled around listening to Mom read.

Later in the day with the sunlight glittering through the windows, I was looking toward Joe's picture. Seeing him dressed in his uniform, I wondered what Mom and Dad would think if I told them I was thinking of joining the army. I've got to do something meaningful, I thought.

"Got another letter to take its place," Dad said, removing the last letter from his bib pocket and putting in its place the letter that arrived earlier in the day.

With the passing of the next couple days, I was thinking more seriously about joining the army. What were my choices? I thought. I'd traveled the road, I'd roughnecked in the oil fields, there was no money for college and I didn't want to work in a mill. That didn't leave much to choose from.

I tried to break the news to Mom and Dad by telling them that in one more year Joe would be home and in three years we'd all be home together.

"Three years is a long time, Son," Mom said as I saw the tears rolling down her cheeks.

Soon I would be leaving.

"Always remember we love you, Son," Dad said.

Chapter 2

---◆---

S addened by my leaving, it took eight weeks for me to complete basic training at Fort Jackson, South Carolina. Sergeant Crawford was our drill sergeant. Quickly I learned not to think for myself but only do as I was told. Danny was a friend of mine. He was a husky Texan from Odessa, not far from where I'd roughnecked in the oil fields. We talked about roughnecking. It was a conversation we understood and could share.

Maybe it was Danny's size, his looks, or that he was a Texan. I don't really know but whatever it was, Sergeant Crawford didn't like him. Danny and I were talking when we saw Sergeant Crawford manhandle one of the guys.

"That's Paul," Danny said in a strong voice.

I could see the angry look in Danny's eyes. "Take it easy, Danny," I called as he started toward them. "Four more weeks and Sergeant Crawford is history." Danny didn't stop.

Paul was sitting on the ground when Sergeant Crawford turned facing Danny. With those husky shoulders pushed upward into the air, Danny looked twice the size of Sergeant Crawford.

---◆---

"You want something, Boy," Sergeant Crawford said to Danny in a strong voice.

Danny didn't say anything. He looked down at Paul then he stood taller than ever, boasting his big frame into the air ready to take on the world.

Sergeant Crawford didn't back down. He knew the army was his strength. "You see that tree, Boy?" Sergeant Crawford asked in a commanding voice.

Danny still didn't say anything.

Paul stood up. "It was my fault, Danny," Paul said.

I knew Paul made his comment trying to protect Danny.

"That tree over there, I said, Do you see it, Boy?"

"I see the tree," Danny replied.

"Do you understand, I'm going to make a soldier out of you, Boy?"

"Yes," Danny replied with his shoulders dropped.

"Yes, Sir, Boy! You're in the army."

"Yes, Sir," Danny replied.

"That's more like it, Boy," Sergeant Crawford said in a very commanding voice. "You know I could have you thrown in the Brig, don't you?"

"Yes, Sir," Danny replied.

"You just remember that." Danny started to walk off. "Come back here, Boy. I didn't tell you you could leave, did I?"

"No, Sir," Danny replied as he quickly returned.

"I asked you, did you see that tree over there?"

"Yes, Sir," Danny replied.

"Yes, Sir is the first thing you learn in the army, Boy. You understand that?"

"Yes, Sir, Sir," Danny replied.

"You're in the army, Boy, and that means you don't think for yourself. You understand that?"

"Yes, Sir," Danny replied.

"Fort Jackson is the army and that tree is part of Fort

Jackson. It's helped to make many a boy like you into a fine soldier. You understand that?"

"Yes, Sir, Sir."

"You're beginning to learn, Boy. You're a Texan and Texans like that tree, don't they?"

"Yes, Sir."

"Well don't stand there, Boy. Say 'Yes, Sir' to that tree for three hours. You understand?"

"Yes, Sir, Sir," Danny replied as he moved toward the tree.

. . . .

The weeks passed. Finally we were standing in formation ready to graduate from basic training. As we listened to Sergeant Crawford, we stood proudly. In a commanding voice, he spoke. "You're soldiers. You're the best. You're part of the team. You represent yourself. You represent me. You represent the United States. You're the army. You're the best. Just remember that."

The ceremony was over. Sergeant Crawford walked over to where Danny was standing. "You're the best," Sergeant Crawford said.

"Yes, Sir," Danny replied proudly.

For eight weeks we were a team, a close-knit group of men. We'd learned to listen, to respond and to say, "Yes, Sir." We'd learned most of all to be soldiers.

I received my orders. I was assigned to the Army Security Agency. After two weeks leave, I would report to Fort Devens, Mass.

I was fully dressed in my uniform, proud and anxious as I hitchhiked heading toward home. Unlike times before, with my uniform on a car quickly pulled over. I reached down and picked up my bag and quickly ran down the road.

"Howdy," I said as I opened the door.

"Howdy," the middle aged gentleman replied.

In a moments time we were on our way. Somewhat relaxed, I was sitting back, anticipating the welcome home.

"Where you heading?" the gentleman asked.

"North Carolina, that's my home," I answered proudly. "I've just finished basic training."

"You're from a good state. My home is North Carolina, too."

"Where?" I asked, anxious to know how close to home he might be going.

"Rockingham."

"Rockingham! That's only about fifty miles from home. I'm from Carthage."

"Guess you're glad to be heading home?"

"Yes, Sir, I sure am. Seems like it's been a long time."

"I know the feeling. I used to be in service too."

Traveling for a while longer the car began to slow down. "Maybe this will help you a little," he said as I opened the door.

"Yes, Sir, it sure does. Thanks a lot."

After catching a couple more rides, I was watching, wide-eyed and excited as I read the sign, Carthage.

"How much further to your home?" the gentleman asked.

"About seven miles. I can make it on in from here."

"It's so late in the evening, if you'd like, I'll take you home."

"Thanks, I appreciate your offer, Sir, but I don't want to cause you any trouble."

"No trouble at all. There was a time I was in service and I know what it's like."

"You sure it's no trouble?"

"None at all. You just show me the way."

I gave the directions. A short time later I could see the metal rooftop of our house. As we drove in I looked across the yard and then out across the field. I was hoping to see Dad. With no one in sight, I picked up my bag and opened the door. "Thanks a lot for the ride, Sir, and for bringing me home."

"Just glad to do it."

"Thanks again, Sir."

"You take care," the gentleman said as I stood watching the rising dust with the car going off.

Then turning, I looked around again still expecting to see Dad. He was nowhere in sight. I just stood waiting—waiting to see him out in the yard—waiting to hear him call my name. But in the silence I finally reached down and picked up my bag and started toward the house. They didn't hear the car. Maybe that's why no one came out, I thought as I stepped up on the porch. Anxious to hear a voice, I knocked on the door. "Dad, it's me, Jim, I'm home," I called. Still there was no sound.

I reached and took hold of the door knob. Giving it a twist, I lifted on the door and pushed it back. Trying to be quiet, I tiptoed inside. There were no voices; not a sound anywhere as I went from one room to the other. Staring at a picture of Mom and Dad, I walked over and picked it up. Holding it in my hand, I couldn't hold the tears back. Placing the picture back, wiping the tears from my eyes, I turned and slowly walked away. Opening the bedroom door, with the sunlight glittering through the window pane, I sat down on the bedside. In the quietness of the hour, like I should hear the voices of Mom and Dad, I sat staring, looking at my rifle where it remained in its usual place, untouched since I last held it.

Thinking that any moment Mom and Dad would walk in, I relaxed as I removed my shoes and lay across the bed. I must have dropped off to sleep as I awakened to the sound of a little movement. It was Mom and Dad. I could hear their voices. Hearing them talk, I could hardly wait to go in. I waited a little longer and then I got up and quietly walked toward the kitchen. "Mama! Daddy!" I said, standing in the doorway.

"Jim! You're home," Dad said excitedly, reaching out to shake my hand.

"We weren't expecting you, Son, not until tomorrow," Mom said as she walked over and hugged me.

"I know, Mom. I just wanted to surprise you. It sure seems good to be home," I said, pulling a chair back, sitting down.

"Cup of coffee, Son?" Dad asked, with a gleam of happiness on his face.

"Sounds good," I answered, feeling the warmth of our closeness, like old times.

"How's that?" Dad asked, pouring my coffee.

"Good. That's plenty, Dad."

"How are things here?" I asked.

"About the same. Everyone seems to be getting along as usual. Sylvia is doing some nurse aid work. She and John ought to be in any time."

. . . .

The two weeks leave passed quickly. It was my last night at home and John and I were lying awake. "John; Mom and Dad, you sure everything is okay with them?"

"They're okay. Sometimes Daddy says it's not like it used to be. Once in a while I see him walking out across the field."

"That doesn't surprise me." He's looking to the future, recalling the past, letting the present go by, I thought. "What about food? I've been sending a little money home but I know it couldn't be enough."

"We're doing okay," John replied.

John and I stopped talking. I knew this was my last night at home as I lay awake looking out the window, seeing the brightness of the moon.

"John," I spoke, thinking that he might be asleep.

"Yeah," he answered.

"If it weren't for Mom and Dad, I wish you were going with me."

"I thought about that when you joined but with Joe in the army and you joining, I knew with Dad's condition I

---

needed to be here. It's just that it is so different now. I miss you and the things we used to get out and do."

"I started to say something to you when I joined but with Dad's condition—I guess that's why I never mentioned it. The old car is here. Why don't you get out and do around some?" I lay waiting, thinking that John would say something, but in the quietness I knew he was thinking. Finally he went to sleep.

With a few hours left, morning soon came. I was ready to leave.

"Bye, Son," Mom and Dad said, when all too soon the sound of their voices were gone. As the bus moved down the road, I looked back seeing Mom and Dad disappear.

"Excuse me," the youthful voice sounded as I looked up.

"Are you speaking to me?" I asked, looking up observing a beautiful girl standing next to me.

"Anyone sitting with you?" she asked.

"No, there's no one sitting with me. Would you like to sit here?"

"You mind?" she asked as I stood up to let her in.

"No, please join me. My name is Jim Boyte," I said as I reached over to shake her hand.

"Darlene is my name."

"Darlene. That's a pretty name for a beautiful lady."

"Thank you. Have you been in the army very long?" she asked, making conversation.

"Not very long. I'm coming off leave on my way to Fort Devens, Mass. What about you, where you heading?"

"I'm on my way to Boston. That's my home."

Soon we would be arriving at Worcester, the place where I would get off. Conversation with Darlene made a pleasant trip. I told her again what a beautiful girl she was and what a pleasure the trip had been. With an invitation to come and see her, she gave me her address and phone number.

"Thanks for the invitation. I'll give you a call."

As I got up she smiled and shook my hand. "Thanks for letting me join you," she said.

I reported in for duty and then with a few hours sleep I was awakened. "Boyte! Boyte!" I heard the voice as someone was shaking me.

"Yes, Sir," I answered as I turned to see the sergeant.

"What do you mean, still in that bunk?"

"I don't know. I didn't mean to be, Sir."

"Don't let it happen again."

"It won't, Sir. I'll make sure of that."

"Just to make sure, I'm going to let you pull an extra duty of KP. You understand."

"Yes, Sir. I understand."

Oversleeping was one mistake too many. It wouldn't happen again. The sergeant didn't tell me but maybe that was why they delayed my testing. In the meantime, since I took typing in high school, I was assigned as a helper to Sergeant Brooks in the personnel office. Sergeant Brooks was a big talker. It didn't take long before he seemed to take a liking to me. We talked about many things—about the army life, about what it would be like to get back to the farm where he too grew up. I told him about Joe being in the army and the closeness that developed between John and me as we grew up, and about how John stayed home because of Dad's condition.

It was late in the evening and the day's work was almost completed. "Jim, I've been thinking," Sergeant Brooks said. "About you and John. Your Dad's condition—you said you and your brothers provided the living for the family as you grew up."

"That's right," I replied.

"I just checked the guidelines. If you can prove you and your brothers provided over fifty percent of the livelihood for your parents, there's government funding available, called the Class Q allotment."

"What do you mean?" I asked with enthusiasm.

"With all three of you in the military at the same time, your parents could receive governmental support. We could hold you in transit here until your brother arrives."

"That sounds good, but do you really think it can be done?"

"I think it's possible. There's special consideration for brothers being together. The main personnel office is in Arlington, Virginia but I think we can handle things from here. You'll need to talk with Captain Whitehead."

"Thanks for letting me know."

The day's work was over and I was lying awake. There was so much to think about. I saw how hard it was on Mom and Dad when Joe joined and John told me what it was like after I left. Still I thought about John and what it would mean for his future, what it would be like for the two of us to have our closeness again.

With little sleep, I walked in the office the next morning. Sergeant Brooks spoke. "Did you decide to stay with us for awhile?" he asked.

"Yes, Sir. If we can get the funding for Mom and Dad."

"I thought that would be your decision. I've already said something to Captain Whitehead. You'll need to talk with him."

"Thanks, Sergeant."

I talked with Captain Whitehead. He said there would be no problem. They would hold me in transit until John arrived. Still I didn't know what to do. Finally I wrote the letter and waited several hours before mailing it.

Several days later I received a letter from John. On the outside of the envelope, I read Private John K. Boyte, Fort Jackson, S.C.

. . . .

In the weeks that followed I began to hear about a place called Sinop, located in a very remote area of Turkey. Soon I was in a dilemma. John was in the army, expecting to join me, and I wanted to go to Sinop. As the weeks passed, with some assurance from Sergeant Brooks and Captain Whitehead that John would get a good assignment not too far from home, I made the decision to go to Sinop, Turkey. With my background in typing, I got an M.O.S. as a clerk.

Writing the letters to Mom, Dad, and John informing them of my decision was not easy. Later I got my orders. John got home from basic training and a few days later I was home on leave. Our days being together as a family were more cherished than ever. The time was drawing near. John was leaving and in a couple of days I would be gone. Finally the time came. We were standing, waiting for the bus to stop in Carthage.

"Here it comes," Dad said.

I watched as Mom and Dad hugged John and then he turned to me.

"I wish you were going with me," he said.

I was at a loss for words. I didn't want to have tears. I quickly reached out and hugged him and then Mom, Dad, and I watched the bus drive off.

I looked at Mom and Dad. Tears were rolling down Mom's cheeks. Dad didn't say anything. I knew he was holding the tears back, that on the inside he was hurting very badly. As we were getting in the car, Dad spoke.

"John was the last of you boys and now he's gone," Dad said.

We were in the car driving home. I wanted to cry but I knew I couldn't. With nothing being said, I just looked over at Mom and Dad. I felt like part of me was gone. I wanted the night before to come back, to be able to talk with John. To talk about the times when the other children went to the cafeteria and we stayed in the classroom hidden in the corner eating our egg biscuits. I wanted to make everything like it used to be, but I couldn't.

"Sure will be glad when you boys get back," Dad said as we turned off the main road.

"We're coming back, Daddy," I said as I looked at the woods where we used to hunt.

"You remember the old hickory tree, Jim Boy?" Dad said pointing toward the tree where I shot my first squirrel.

"I'll always remember it, Dad, and when I get back we'll hunt again."

"Those were some good times," Dad said as he looked over at Mom. "We always enjoyed you fellows. It seems like only yesterday when Mom was making those little dresses and putting them on you."

When we drove in the yard, Mom and I went into the house while Dad walked out toward the field. I watched Mom as she walked over and picked up John's picture. I didn't say anything as I glanced out the window and saw Dad standing near the edge of the field. Then I looked back at Mom.

"Son, we want you to write us often. It'll mean so much to your dad and to all of us."

"I will, Mom. It's just that I've always had difficulty in writing, but I'll do better."

"Your letters mean so much to us, Son."

I looked out the window and saw Dad walking toward the old chicken house. "Mom, if anything happens to Dad be sure to let me know."

"Before your dad was hurt, he worked hard. He wanted to provide for you children."

"I know, Mom," I said as I started out to where he was.

"I was just looking at the weeds in the field and the leaking roof on the chicken house, thinking about how much I wanted it to be different," Dad said as I walked up to him.

"Don't worry about the fields and the old chicken house, Dad. When I get out of the army and John and Joe are here, we'll have that tractor and we'll fix the farm up like you planned for us before you were hurt."

"I can't do much," Dad said but I'll be waiting for you.

"I'll get a turn of wood," I said as we started in the house.

. . . . .

The next two days passed quickly and it was my last night at home. I was lying awake hoping the next three years would pass quickly. Into the hours of the night I lay unable to sleep. I knew Dad was awake. He always snored when he was sleeping. Knowing my time with Mom and Dad was drawing nigh, I got up and quietly walked to their doorway. They didn't see me as I stood in the darkness. Dad, I thought, I wonder what you are thinking? We're grown now, it's like it happened overnight without time to adjust.

Finally I went into their room and set on the side of the bed. With the brightness of the moon, I could see Dad as he turned to face me.

"Someday, Dad, I'm coming back. We'll plow the fields and clear more land. It'll be like we've always wanted it."

"I can't do much," Dad replied. "But we'll be waiting for you. I think often times of how many years ago I'd come in from work. You children would be asleep, but I'd always go in and look at each of you. I'd even look to make sure you were breathing okay. You're grown now and I can't watch over you like that. Many times when you all are gone, I think how wonderful it would be if I knew each of you were okay.

"Jim," Dad continued, "you see the moon up there?"

"Yeah, Dad."

"When you're overseas and looking up at it, remember I'm looking at it with you and thinking about you boys. The world is big and you're facing it, Son. Always love as we have loved one another. Treat your fellow man good and always remember the difference between right and wrong."

"Don't worry about those things, Dad. You and Mom have given your life to us. The love you've given will never cease. You've taught us right from wrong. We'll go forth giving as you have given unto us."

"Always remember, Jim, we love you."

"Try to get some sleep, Dad," I said cherishing each of the remaining moments. Then I said good-night, realizing it would be a long time before I would say good-night again. Dad looked at me as I walked out.

I didn't sleep much. The next morning I was up early walking through the fields when I heard Dad call.

"Come on, Jim Boy. The bus will soon be there."

"Here, Son, take this with you," Mom said, handing me a Bible.

"Thanks, Mom."

"Be sure and read it. It has all the words of comfort."

"You got everything?" Dad asked as we were about to get in the car.

"Everything is here," I answered, putting my duffel bag in the trunk. Taking one last look as we were driving off, I knew the time of growing up was gone.

"Jim, take this with you," Dad said, handing me his harmonica as the bus came into sight.

"But it's yours, Dad," I replied, taking it in my hand.

"I want you to have it, Son," he said.

"The bus, it's here, Son," Mom said as the bus was driving up.

"I love you," I said as I boarded the bus.

Chapter 3

———◆———

Travel by bus from home to Charleston, S.C. only took a few hours. Soon we were on the plane enroute to Ankara, Turkey. With stops in Bermuda, the Azores, Tripoli, and Athens we finally arrived at the airport in Ankara. After reporting to headquarters, I went out for a walk. We were told to enjoy the evening before making the trip next day to Sinop. It was a sunshiny afternoon with a gentle breeze and a few clouds drifting in the sky. There were people everywhere and no voices to understand. Off at a little distance, rising upward into the sky, were rough, rugged mountains. No one paid me much attention. Horns were honking. Some little children came running up to me. "Ciklet," they said holding out their hands, but I didn't understand. I reached in my pocket and showed them I didn't have any goodies. "Hey, Joe," a woman called to me. I turned and looked and then I thought it best that I go on.

I kept walking, unafraid. I wanted to walk on toward the barren mountain. The emptiness it held seemed to engulf my life. A little ways further I stopped to watch a herder with his sheep crossing the road. For several minutes I stood relaxed. No one, not even the sheep were paying me any

———◆———

attention. The sheepherder finally looked in my direction and gave a little nod. Then suddenly a car came roaring down the road, screeching its wheels as it came to an abrupt stop just a few feet from the sheep. I kept watching in awe the calmness of the aged herder guiding his sheep while he totally ignored the angry frustrations of the young driver yelling and honking his horn. A few minutes later when the sheep were safely across the road, I stood watching the frail herder with his cane unmoved by the angry yelling of the young driver as he swiftly sped away.

Later as I was nearing headquarters I stopped to talk with a couple of G.I.'s. "When did you come aboard?" they asked, apparently thinking I just arrived.

"Today," I replied.

"Where's your assignment?"

"Sinop. I'll be there for one year."

"Luck to you! That's one year too long," came the response.

"You must know something about Sinop?"

"Too much. That's where we've lost one year of our lives. You'll find out what it's like when you get there."

Listening as they talked, I didn't say much. I learned most of what they were saying back at Fort Devens. We were up early the next morning, ready to move out. Unlike Simms and Duvone, I asked to come and was anxious to see what was ahead. With our baggage loaded, we got on back of the truck and were on our way. For a distance of approximately twenty miles the riding was smooth. Then all at once the dust rolled in. Soon the roaring of the engine became louder as the truck began to pull harder, moving us upward into the mountains. Boredom came quickly as we traveled the barren mountains, empty of life, replaced only by rocks and jagged crevices. Later in the evening I knew night was approaching as a redness shone from the sun draping through the clouds. Then going into the darkness, I sat viewing the moon, clutching Dad's harmonica in my hand. We traveled up and down the mountains for eighteen hours. Then finally we started up the last mountain, the place that was to be home for one year. Anxious to get some sleep, we patiently waited for someone to issue our bedding.

"Silverware too?" Duvone asked as the blankets and sheets were issued.

"That's part of it," the supply clerk said, giving each of us silverware.

May be some changes later, we were told, but for the time being Simms, Duvone, and I were assigned to Hut A.

"Anybody else in Hut A?" Simms asked.

"Yeah. A guy by the name of Duke. He's been here for a while. Bring your things on. I'll show you where you're staying."

"Here. This is Hut A," he said and then walked off, leaving us standing at the door.

"You guys just get in?" Duke asked, turning over, waking to our noise.

"We just got here," Duvone answered.

So this is our hut, I thought, staring at the canvas, feeling the coldness with the fire in the potbelly heater gone out.

There was not much sleep as early in the morning I awakened to Duke's movements. "You been here very long, Duke," I asked.

"Four months and thirteen days," he answered as I recalled the comments of so many, counting from one day to the next.

"That's a pretty good while," I replied, crawling out from under my blankets. "This place as bad as I've heard?"

"That all depends on how well you can pass time doing nothing. One thing for sure, there's not much to do."

Quickly dressing, I stepped outside, anxious to see for myself all that I'd heard. In the calmness of the air, standing atop the mountain, there were no trees anywhere. The sun was shining brightly and almost everywhere I looked the land was surrounded by the Black Sea. Walking on, looking downward, I could see the passageway through which we traveled.

"Howdy," one of the fellows spoke, carrying his silverware.

"Howdy," I replied.

With only the bareness of the mountain and no trees and the quonset huts placed in a semicircular shape, it looked so desolate. I began to realize, as the next several days passed, the adventure I left John for was twelve months of isolation and loneliness, sitting, waiting to go home. I developed a closeness of friendship with Shane and Gary. Another G.I. by the name of Tom became a close friend, but in conversation didn't have much to say.

"Are you turning in so early?" Shane asked as I was leaving the club.

"I might as well, tonight is not my night. You fellows finish out the game."

"Ah, come on, we got to have somebody to beat, "Gary said, smiling.

"Another day, Gary, I'll show you how to play."

Stepping out into the darkness, I listened to the surging waves as they crashed inland. A short time later I was alone, sitting on my bunk, holding a picture of Mom and Dad. *I know you all want to hear from me, Mom. I promised you I'd do better but it's still so hard to write. More often than not I'd rather crawl in the bunk and try to pass time sleeping. It's too cold to write, Mom, you'd understand if you were here.* Then crawling in under the blankets, I felt the coldness against my body as I lay awake thinking. "Just write us often, Son, that'll mean so much to us," I remembered Mom saying. It was just too much, I had to get up and write the letter.

Dear Mom, Dad, and Sylvia,

The trip is over and I'm settled in. Many hours were spent flying across the ocean. The last part of the trip was made by truck from Ankara to here.

Haven Reformed Church Library
5350 North 25th Street
Kalamazoo, Michigan 49004

I hope all of you are feeling well. As for me, I'm doing fine. I don't want you to worry about me.

Have you heard from John lately. I hated to leave him but maybe it's for the best. Often times I think about him and wish we were together.

Dad, thanks for the harmonica . . . .

I continued writing, having a feeling of comfort as the words of conversation went on. Finally when the letter was completed, I felt better, ready for some sleep.

A week later, on Saturday afternoon at approximately 1400 hours, I sat alone on the side of my bunk, gazing at the canvas and listening to the rumbling of the fire in the pot belly heater. Earlier in the day I was at the club gaining more experience about life on the mountain.

The club was known as home away from home, an old wooden frame building with two windows, one door and ten tables. It was a place of refuge from the sergeants and the officers and even refuge from the canvas covered huts. It was well known that the building was built by the enlisted men, EM men as we were known, those of us with less rank than sergeants or officers, most often known as those who would serve for one enlistment and then get out.

I had been sitting at one of the ten tables, playing cards and listening to the war stories. Anyone who has been around soldiers knows that there are always war stories, the stories of the old days, the days that never die. Bill was sitting across from me and even though I wasn't drinking, he, like the others, were quick to accept me. I knew from their voices and the desiring look in their eyes I brought something special for the moment. I brought a feeling of closeness to home, I was new to the mountain.

A few minutes later I stoked the fire and walked down on the mountain side. There I took my place next to the sea. It was a cool evening with a gentle breeze blowing and there was a calmness to the waves like a bird gently gliding through the air. I was experiencing a fullness of life, something that I learned in growing up only God could give. I pulled my harmonica out and started playing and a few minutes later I heard a faint voice call, startling me as I looked back. Unsure at first, I waited before speaking.

"Tom, it's you. I didn't recognize your voice. How did you know I was down here?"

"I went by your hut, Duke said he thought you'd gone out walking."

"Do you come down here very often?" I asked, seeing that he had Gimp, the dog, and a couple Turkish boys with him.

"Every few days. It's become a way of life for me. I suppose you might say a way of passing time. I first started to hit the bottle but soon realized that wasn't for me. I was just getting drunk like all the rest.

"The Turkish boys usually around, Tom?"

"Sometimes. There's usually several of the kids but these two are my buddies. I've known them for a good while."

Looking at the boys with Gimp in their joyful play, the leisure of the evening passed. Then Tom and I stood watching the boys disappear, going into the distance.

"They're brothers," Tom said, speaking solemnly as we turned and started up the mountain. "Taner is the oldest. You probably noticed him speaking some English, but my favorite is Mehmet, the little one."

"How old are they?"

"I'm not sure, probably around eight and ten."

"Gimp, it's you. You decided to come back," I said reaching down, rubbing his fur as we were nearing the top of the mountain.

. . . .

More than two weeks passed. Surely Mom got my letter, I thought, as I went out to mail call. Finally my name was called. Anxiously I opened the letter.

Dear Son,

We were so glad to get your letter and learn that everything is okay with you. I kept wanting to write you but didn't have your address.

We are all doing pretty well. Dad often times speaks about you boys. Occasionally I see him out walking across the field. You know how much he was hoping you could farm. Just last night he was talking about it . . .

Remember, Son, we all love you and hope that we will be hearing from you very often.

All of our love,
Mom, Dad, Sylvia

I folded the letter and placed it in my pocket. At a distance I saw Tom walking. Hurriedly I took off, "Tom, wait up," I called. "Tom! Hey, Tom, wait up." Suddenly he turned around.

"That you calling?" he asked.

"Yeah. What's your hurry?"

"There's no hurry. I first started to wait on you but you were reading your letter."

"What about you? Did you get a letter?"

"There was nothing for me, but that's not unusual," Tom said stooping down, rubbing Gimp's fur. Tom seemed lonely, a loneliness different from the rest.

. . . .

For most of the G.I.'s, living on the mountain with an occasional stroll down through the village of Sinop was a life of existence, waiting to go home. I listened and watched the old-timers, they weren't hard to identify as they carried their short-timer's sticks. In a proud voice and with a subtle smile, like a major accomplishment happened. "I've added another notch," they'd say, holding out their stick. Then the smile would disappear and something of advice would come.

"The year will go by. You'll find a way to sleep, to drink, and to go out walking," they'd say.

Early on Saturday morning a few of us were out walking. The wind was blowing and there was a briskness of cool air coming in off the sea. The sun was up a ways and a few clouds were drifting in the sky. We were approximately halfway down the mountain when one of the trucks passed by and one of the old-timers going home waved and tossed his short-timer's stick to us. We kept walking with no destination, like an abandoned ship drifting at sea.

"So soon," Gary commented, seeing some children moving in our direction.

Listening to their voices, "Ciklet," they called as I remembered the children in Ankara.

"They can be pesky," Gary said, not paying them much attention.

I saw the smiles as Tom reached in his pocket and handed each of them a piece of chewing gum.

"That's all they wanted," Tom said, smiling, reaching over patting one of the little fellows on the head.

"You guys coming?" Gary called from a distance.

"What's your hurry, Gary? What are you going to do when we get there?" Shane asked, smiling, almost laughing.

"I just like to keep moving," Gary said as we were walking through Sinop.

"You've got ten and a half months to get there," Shane replied.

"You can't count, Shane. It's only ten months and eight days."

"If there were some girls around it'd make life so much easier," Shane said.

"Don't strain your eyes, Shane," Gary remarked with a grin.

There was not a female anywhere. There were only the men sitting at little tables, drinking hot tea and playing dominoes. No horns were honking, there was just the movement of people along the streets. We kept walking, going beyond Sinop. Along the way we met an old Turkish man guiding his oxen hitched to a cart. At a distance of approximately twenty feet behind the cart an old Turkish woman wearing a veil was carrying wood on her back. We kept walking, passing the time. Finally we turned and started in.

"Walk, walk, walk! That's all we can do here," Gary said.

"I tell you what's wrong, Gary," Shane said, pointing to the sea. "There it is, and we can't cross it."

. . . .

It was a month later. I was sitting on my bunk staring at the calendar where I'd marked the days off.

"Come on! Let's go. We've got another mail call," Duke said, speaking excitedly. Waiting for the mail to be sorted, we all stood around watching for the wooden shutters to open.

"No mail for you, Jim," Shane said, walking over to where I was standing.

"You seen Tom?" I asked.

"Yeah, he's standing over yonder."

Suddenly the shutters opened. I anxiously waited. "Olson," I heard the name called as I watched Shane smiling, reaching for his letter. A lot of names were called. I was still standing, waiting and hoping. Finally, the words I didn't want to hear. That's all fellows, as I watched the window shutters close.

"I was joking you about the letter," Shane said, turning to me.

"I'll make up for it next time, " I replied, turning in the direction of Tom. "There'll be another mail call, Tom," I said, realizing that neither of us received a letter.

"There's always another mail call," Tom replied as we walked off.

"There they are, Tom, the two boys," I said, watching Gimp running to them.

"Look at Mehmet, Jim, the little one. Every now and then, if you'll notice, you'll see that he has difficulty walking."

Tom was right. I hadn't noticed the limp very much before.

"I don't know what's wrong," Tom said. "Sometimes I think he's getting better, but other times he seems to be weaker."

I looked over at Tom, his youthful look with his strawberry blonde hair and his six foot, slender frame. He seemed so close and yet so distant. Maybe it was his loneliness and his love for the children that made him different.

"Mehmet!" Tom called, throwing a little ball to him.

I watched the ball slip through Mehmet's hands as he quickly reached down and picked it up. Just as I thought he was going to throw it to Tom, "Em," he said, tossing it in my direction.

I smiled and tossed it back.

"You see what I mean?" Tom said as we watched him stumble, trying to catch the ball.

I kept watching Mehmet and Taner. There was something special about each of them. Their closeness as brothers and their closeness to Tom was different from all the other children.

Finally the sun was setting and the boys were gone down the mountain.

Back in the hut I sat on my bunk waiting for another day to come. With thoughts of going to the club and getting drunk, I thought back to Dad; back to the things he and Mom taught me. It's not all a bowl of cherries, Dad. Like you said, the world is big and I'm facing it.

"Jim, over here," Simms called as I opened the door to the club.

"Room for another player?"

"Only because it's you," Ted said as I pulled the chair back.

"What're you drinking?" Simms asked, ordering another round of beers.

"A coke. I'm still not old enough for anything stronger," I replied, passing it off as a joke.

"Come on, Jim. You can't stay a Young'un all your life," Ted remarked.

"Better have one," Simms said.

"Maybe later," I replied, seeing that early in the evening Simms was already feeling the effects.

We played awhile longer. Finally with it getting late I decided to turn in.

"You got our money, now you leaving," Simms said.

"I just had a little luck, that's all."

"That you, Jim?" Duke asked as I opened the door.

"Yeah," I answered quietly, trying not to disturb Duvone.

"Is Simms on his way?" Duvone asked, turning over in his bunk.

"He was at the club when I left."

"Another one of those nights," Duvone replied.

About two hours later the door opened and in stumbled Simms. "Jim," Simms called. "Jim," he called again.

"What is it, Simms?" I answered.

"That you, Jim?"

"Yeah! It's me."

"Turn the light on. I've been to three different huts trying to get here."

"It's okay, Simms. You're back in your hut."

"Can't you turn the light on?"

"No problem, Simms. You're doing okay."

"You going to wake me in the morning, aren't you?"

"Damn it, Simms. Go to sleep," Duvone yelled.

"Jim, You going to get me up?" Simms asked again.

"No problem, Simms. We'll get you up."

Soon Simms was snoring, dead to the world. I lay in

the darkness looking out the window, seeing only the stars, having thoughts that someday I would be going home.

The rising and the setting of the sun was like the swinging pendulum of a clock. Changing only time with little to remember it by. The wind was blowing and I was sitting on my bunk, hearing the vibrations of the canvas, watching Duke cut another notch in his short-timer's stick. "How many days, Duke?" I asked, knowing it couldn't be too many.

"Sixty-two. How 'bout you? How many you got left?"

"Too many. I've still got a long time to go," I replied as Duke stood up.

"You coming?" Duke asked as he left to go to the club.

"Maybe later. I need to write a letter."

Duke was gone. I sat alone staring at the canvas. Then I reached over and picked up my last letter from Mom and Dad. "Your dad and I want to hear from you often, Son," Mom said as I read it again.

"I know, Mom. I'm sorry. It's like the Bible you gave me. I brush the dust off of it once in awhile but never get around to reading it anymore. You see, Mom, we're a drinking bunch, just passing time, all waiting to go home." I sat on, looking at my Bible, thinking about what Mom said. Finally I reached over and picked up the Bible and started reading. Just as I placed the Bible down, I heard a knock.

"Something wrong, Tom?" I asked as he walked in.

"Nothing really. Just one of those times," Tom said and then he paused. "Don't know whether you're interested but the Chaplain drove in this evening."

"The Chaplain? I was looking at my Bible a few minutes ago, thinking about how I used to go to church."

"I've got a Bible too, but I don't read it anymore," Tom said.

The Chaplain held service the next morning and later in the evening there was a second service. A passing comment that we might consider building a small chapel interested me.

Chapter 4

---◆---

The Chaplain came, giving us the Word of God. Then he departed, leaving us on the mountain with no place to go, not even a rooftop where we could seek shelter in silent meditation. But his spoken words were like a moving force. He challenged us, stimulating conversation in Bible study, leading us to talk about everything from building a little one room chapel to a very large structure. While the idea of building a chapel was of interest, the obstacles were many, ranging from being in a Moslem country to being in the military. Yet, God is everywhere we knew and His work goes on. A few weeks passed. I didn't mean to mislead anyone about my knowledge of building, but knowing that the power of God working through His people can do anything, I stood, somewhat nervous, waiting to go in the major's office.

"Sir, Private First Class Boyte would like to see you," Sergeant Randall said.

"Send him in," I heard the major say.

Stepping into the major's office I watched his expression as I snapped to attention.

---◆---

"You wanted to see me?" the major asked in a somewhat stern voice.

"Yes, Sir. Sir, several of us have been having Bible study weekly. We've talked about the possibility of building a chapel, something that would be temporary. In addition to having a place for Bible study, it would give us all something to do while we are here."

"I see," the major said. "But in particular, what do you have in mind?"

"We were wondering, Sir, if you would be willing to let us build the chapel," I replied. Then I waited, anticipating his response.

"No more often than the chaplain gets up, do you think you really need it?"

"It's just that we want to build it, Sir."

"I see and where've you been meeting?"

"Different places, Sir. When it's pretty weather we usually meet over on the mountainside."

"And how many of you fellows are there?"

"There's eight to twelve of us, Sir. It varies from time to time."

"Eight to twelve, so you're talking about a small building."

"Yes, Sir. A place for Bible study and something to do while we're building it."

"What about the material? How would you manage that?"

"We're not sure, Sir. We first wanted to know if you would approve it. If you will, some way we'll get it built."

Again the major waited. Finally he spoke, "I don't know, Boyte. Do you know anything about building?"

"Yes, Sir. I've got some knowledge of building. There'd be no problem with that."

"It's not a bad idea."

"You mean we can build it?"

"Let me think about it for a week. You know that we're

in a Moslem country and we don't want to cause any problems."

"Yes, Sir. And you do want me to come back in a week?"

"That'll be fine. I'll have an answer for you then."

"Thank you, Sir." Snapping to attention, I gave a salute and left. Shane was waiting for me on the outside.

"What did the old man have to say?" Shane asked.

"He listened and asked me several questions and then he told me to come back in a week."

"Do you think he'll let us build it?"

"I don't know. The way he was talking, he seemed to be concerned that we might cause problems with the Turks."

"You mean because they're Muslims?"

"Yeah, that's what he said."

"So he probably won't let us build it."

"I don't know. He'll let us know in a week."

"At least he didn't say no."

We were walking along when Shane stopped. "I was just thinking," Shane said. "Suppose he does let us build it, where do you think we ought to put it?"

"Maybe over there," I replied.

"Over there! That close to the N.C.O. Club? You know how that would go over."

. . . .

Throughout the week I kept thinking about the chapel and about what Mom and Dad said—"You've accepted Christ, now always let Him be your leader."

"You back again?" Sergeant Randall asked.

"Yes, Sir. The major asked me to come back in a week."

"Sir, Private First Class Boyte is here. Said that you asked him to come back in a week."

"Send him in," I heard the major say.

Stepping into the major's office I snapped to attention and saluted.

"You asked that I come back in a week, Sir."

———◢———

"Yes, that's right. It was the chapel we were talking about."

"Yes, Sir, it was."

"And how many did you say wanted to build it?"

"There's about twelve of us, Sir."

"Does that mean there's twelve?"

"There's usually eight to twelve of us, Sir, that meet together."

"I like the idea of building the chapel. It's just that we can't do anything that would cause problems. You understand, don't you?"

"Yes, Sir. I understand. It's just that we believe there is a need for it."

"Have you all decided how large you want to build it?"

"No, Sir, not yet. But if you'll let us build it we won't cause any problems and I'll assure you that you'll be proud of it." Again I waited, wondering what the major's decision would be. Finally he spoke.

"I guess it'll be okay. Just remember that we're in a Moslem country. We're here at their invitation."

"Thank you, Sir, and like I told you, you'll be proud of it when it's finished."

"I'll be watching. I'm sure you'll do your best."

"Yes, Sir. Like I said, you'll be pleased."

Returning to where Shane and I previously stood, I paused, letting my thoughts be with God.

We can't do it alone, God, not the kind of chapel we plan to build. We're in the military located in a Moslem country and we have no money or materials. I told the major he'd be proud of it, but more importantly, God, we want You to be proud of it. I pray that we may always allow Your presence to be with us, enabling Your power to work through us so that we may move forward.

I turned and walked off a distance. Then viewing the

magnitude of the sea, my thoughts returned to the warmth of home, the place where I gained my experience in building our log house. *Daddy, it's still such a long time before I'll be coming home, but one of these days I'll be back. Right now though we've got work to do. We're going to build a chapel. I know all the enjoyment that was ours together, now I'm going to share this with you as we go along.*

"Gimpy, boy, where's Tom? I've got some news for him."

Chapter 5

A couple of weeks passed. It was night time and we were at the club, joking and carrying on as usual when Ted made his comment. "What's this rumor about a chapel, Jim?"

Surprised by Ted's tone of voice, I looked over at him, "It's not a rumor, Ted. We're going to build a chapel."

"You've got to be kidding," Ted said in a half joking voice.

"No. I'm not kidding. Don't take us wrong. We're not trying to be overly religious or anything like that but we are planning to build a chapel."

"Come on, Ted. Get off the Young'un's back. There's nothing wrong with building a chapel," Bill said.

"I didn't mean anything by it, Jim. You know how I am when I'm loaded."

"You don't have to apologize, Ted," Shane remarked.

We played on and then just as I was ready to leave I looked over at Ted.

"What's wrong, Ted? Can't you make it?" Gary asked as we were watching him trying to stand up.

"Look who's talking," Ted replied, almost stumbling with a big grin on his face.

I was on my way out when I heard Bill's voice.

"Not there, Ted! Wait! Go outside," Bill said, speaking loudly.

I turned and looked back.

Bills words fell on deaf ears. Ted stood up and unzipped his pants and let go on the floor. That did it. The game was over.

Through the darkness I walked back to my hut. Along the way I thought about what Ted said and wondered what it would be like trying to build the chapel. "How was your day, Duke?" I asked, as I sat down on my bunk.

"It was okay, but not anything to brag about. I just cut another notch in my short-timer's stick. Forty-five more and that'll be it. How was your day?"

"It was okay, but like you said, nothing to brag about. I was just sitting here thinking, Duke. You know every time you cut a notch in that stick, that means one less day for me."

. . . .

Several days passed. There was still interest in the chapel, but nothing more than talk took place. Some were saying there was no need to build it. Others were saying that because of the number of men, there was no need for building a large chapel. Still others liked the idea of building a large chapel that might someday be permanent.

"Tom, wait up," I called, seeing him at a distance. Soon Tom and I were walking along together. "About the chapel, Tom, have you given it much thought?"

"You mean building it so that someday it might be permanent?"

"That's what we're talking about. What do you think?"

"I haven't given it much thought. Like I told you before, my knowledge of building is not much, but whatever you all want to do, I'm with you."

"But what do you think, Tom?"

"I don't know. Building it large enough to be permanent might take too long. You know I'm leaving in about two months. It's just whatever you all decide. I'm with you."

Tom and I walked on, not saying much. He pulled out the harmonica that was Dad's and started blowing. I just listened, enjoying each moment as we walked on. "There they are," Tom said as I could see the boys coming across the mountain. As they got closer, I watched the smile on Tom's face.

"They're my boys," Tom said.

They didn't have to ask for ciklet. Tom reached in his pocket and gave each of them a piece of gum. Before long Tom, the boys and I walked down next to the sea. A gentle breeze was blowing. The sun was setting, giving a sparkling light that shone across the water. Across the way I could see an old man plowing with his team of oxen. Soon the joyful play came to an end.

"I've enjoyed those little fellows," Tom said as they headed off and we turned and started up the mountain.

"If we build it, any idea how soon we'll start?" Tom asked as we were nearing the top of the mountain.

"Right away, if we expect to get it built," I replied.

Tom didn't say anything else about the chapel. He reached down and started rubbing Gimp's fur. "Old Gimpy reminds me of the only dog I ever had," Tom said in a soft-spoken voice. I waited a moment before speaking.

"How's that, Tom?" I finally asked.

"A long time ago an old stray dog came around. At first he was shabby and not very pretty, more hungry than anything else. Then I began to feed him and he got pretty like Gimp. I named him Old Blue. He was my friend."

"Whatever happened to him?"

"He got run over. I trained him to go get the ball and bring it back. Then one day I threw the ball too hard. It went in the highway and Old Blue never made it. He never came back."

Tom stopped talking. I knew he needed a closeness of friendship, something that seemed to be so distant from him.

. . . .

It took a couple more days to make the final decision. We were going to build the chapel seventy-six feet long and thirty-one feet wide. I was lying awake looking out the window.

"Something wrong?" Duvone asked.

"I'm just having difficulty going to sleep. All my turning, I didn't mean to be bothering you," I replied as I crawled out from under the blankets.

"You weren't bothering me. I was just lying awake. You're not leaving, are you?"

"I'll be back before long," I replied as I closed the door.

I walked out to the barren spot near the N.C.O. Club, the place we mentioned for the chapel. Then as I viewed the moon in all of its splendor, I looked over picturing the chapel, seeing its beauty standing high on the mountain. In a moment of meditation, I bowed my head.

God, we're here passing time, spending a year of loneliness on this mountain. In our weaknesses and difficulties I pray that we may always let Thy guidance be upon us. And now, God, I pray that our minds may be open and receptive to Thy word, enabling us to overcome our weaknesses, doing Thy will as we move forward in building Your chapel. God, you know that my knowledge of building is limited; so I pray that You will grant me wisdom and knowledge as it is needed. Let me be able to have peace of mind, knowing that Your will is always being done.

With a feeling of closeness to God, I felt relaxed as I walked down the mountain.

"Gimpy, old boy, I've just talked with God and we're going to build a large chapel. One that will be beautiful and hopefully for years to come, standing high on this mountain. How's this, old boy?" I said rubbing his fur, taking time to sit down. With Gimp's head rested in my lap, I felt the warmth of my surroundings. I enjoyed the few minutes that followed as I viewed the heavens above and listened to the roaring of the sea. Then as I began to feel the coldness of the air penetrating my clothing, I stood up. "Come on, Gimpy, we've got to go in. We've got to get some sleep." I was being careful not to awaken anyone as I opened the door and quietly walked over to my bunk. With the plans drawn for such a large chapel, questions were asked. Where would the material come from? Who would pay for it? How long would it take to build it? Could we build such a large chapel in a Moslem country? With each of us performing our duties, when would there be time to build it? These were all valid questions. Could the chapel be built?

To the question of money, while it seemed impossible with such a few men, a replica of the chapel was built to be placed in the monthly pay line for contributions. To the question of time, if we could get the chapel started, others who came would complete it.

We had made the decision to build a chapel that might someday become permanent and stand for years to come as a token of the desire of men to bring their loneliness unto God.

It was that time of year when the sun was setting early in the evening, leaving us with little daylight to see by. Finally we started working. First we located a definite site near the N.C.O. Club. Then we laid off the foundation and started digging. With an apparent anxiousness to move ahead in full swing, it was a little surprising to hear William say, "We'll never get it done."

Then Shane responded, "We'll get used to it William. It's just going to take time."

We worked on for a few more minutes and then stopped and headed over to get chow. Later in the evening I walked down to the club. Just as I opened the door, Bill called, "Get you something to drink and come on. We got to get this game underway."

"Come on, Young'un. Aren't you ever going to grow up?" Ted asked seeing the coke in my hand.

I didn't say anything as we all gathered around and started the game.

"So you're going to build the chapel, are you, Young'un?" Ted remarked a few minutes later.

I looked over at Bill as he began to speak. "It's not only the Young'un, it's all of us, Ted. We all need it and we're all going to build it. We'll have a replica of the chapel placed in the pay line and you'll pay your part, too," Bill said.

Watching the frowning expression on Ted's face, I was surprised when he never said anything. For the rest of the evening the conversation was typical as the game went on. Like usual, there was the occasional jabbing at one another, sometimes making it appear that a fight was ready to start.

Later Sunday afternoon Gary and I walked to the chapel site. "Some of us have been talking," Gary said. "There are so many obstacles in the way. We were talking about the size of the chapel, wondering if we might ought to reduce it and build a smaller one. What do you think?" Gary asked.

"I don't know. If that's what you all think. Like I said before, it's not my decision. It's ours with God."

"But really, as large as we're trying to build it, do you think it'll ever be finished?"

"I think it will. But that's just my opinion."

"But look at all the money it's going to take, Jim, and there's only a few of us working on it."

"I still think it can be done, but like I said, that's just my opinion."

"You're confident, aren't you?"

"Yes, I am. I'm confident that even with all the obstacles, if we let God guide us, the chapel will be here serving all those to come in the years ahead."

"It's just that when we get to looking and talking, it seems like an impossibility, but when I see your confidence, I begin to think otherwise," Gary replied.

"But it's like I told you Gary. It's got to be our decision. If it's ever built, however large, it can only be done one way. It's got to be a team with God."

Just as we were about to leave, Shane walked up. I listened to the conversation between Shane and Gary. I didn't say anything. Whatever we did I wanted it to be our decision and not mine. When we walked off I heard Shane say, "If it's ever finished, the way we've planned it, it will stand as a monument to God built by a group of lonely G.I.'s."

Chapter 6

---◆---

K nowing we had the major's approval and some definite plans completed, I left the club early on Tuesday night and went back to my hut. After reading one of Mom's letters again I reached down and picked up my Bible and started reading. Being comforted in God's word, I finished reading and then walked over to the chapel site. There I stood alone in darkness, a far distance from home as I thought about what Mom said when she handed me the Bible. "Be sure to read it. It has all the words of comfort," she said. *Thanks, Mom. I'm a long way from home but you can rest knowing that we are both with God.*

It was the next evening and several of us were at the chapel site. The wind was blowing and out across the sea a brilliant redness shone as the sun was fading away. I walked over to the same spot where I stood the night before, hoping that again I could experience God's presence in the same way. Then I turned and watched the enthusiasm of Henry as he lifted the mattock into the air. The sweat was popping out and the muscles were bulging as he swung the mattock downward, thrusting it into the ground. Then I looked at

---◆---

Shane with the same kind of enthusiasm as he began to shovel the dirt out.

"We've got problems," Henry said as I heard the shrill noise of the mattock striking against the rock.

I looked at the rock. Knowing that the digging was not easy, I took the mattock and began to swing. For the next thirty minutes the motion of the mattock was like the surging waves of the sea, rising upward and then swiftly falling. Then when twilight came and the digging stopped there was silence.

"It's tough going, but we'll get it," Shane said as we walked off.

It was tough. We all had blisters to show for it.

Time was taking us through a rigid monotonous cycle. For most everyone it involved a rotating work schedule of listening and receiving every possible signal from the Soviet Union. Beyond the work schedule there was sleeping and eating and then for everyone there was time left, time that must pass in getting from one day to the next. For most it had meant going to the club with nothing else to do, but now there was something more. There was the building of the chapel.

. . . .

It was another day and we were back at the chapel site.

"Jim, only you, me and Tom. Wonder where the rest are?" Shane asked as we continued to break through the rock.

"I'm not sure, Shane," I replied, beginning to feel a few drops of rain falling.

"But everyone was so excited in the beginning."

"I know, but that excitement is gone, Shane. Digging through these rocks is no excitement. Look at those blisters on your hands."

"Yeah. Look at my blisters," Shane said holding out his hand. "These things hurt when they bust. I guess that's why the other guys are not here."

"We can't count on our few men being here every day, but we'll get it done," I replied.

"If we had some girls here. You know some cheerleaders to cheer us on," Shane said with a smile.

With night coming on, Shane left us to do some other things, leaving only Tom and me to do the digging. I looked over at Tom. He kept swinging the mattock, almost like he was enjoying it.

"You know I'll be leaving you before long. I just wish I had a little more time to help you," Tom said as he pulled the harmonica out and started blowing.

I took a moment of time to enjoy the music as I walked to where the front of the chapel would be.

"Tom," I spoke, interrupting his playing. "I was just looking at this corner, wondering if maybe we should put in a cornerstone."

"A cornerstone?" Tom replied.

"Yeah. Where a Bible and a small American flag could be enclosed and when it's finished the beginning date of the chapel could be engraved."

"That sounds like a good idea," Tom said.

We were still talking about the cornerstone when at a distance, we heard several shrill yelps from Gimp. Quickly Tom and I ran in his direction. As we got closer I saw one of our trucks and the driver was on the outside, stooped over Gimp.

"Jim, look! It's Gimp. He's hurt," Tom said anxiously getting down next to him.

Tom was right. Gimp appeared to be hurt badly. He was lying flat on the ground with little movement, and blood was oozing out from the upper part of his hind leg. I wasn't sure if he were stunned, possibly going into shock, or maybe that he was near the point of death. I watched the painful expression on Tom's face as he reached over to touch him. "Gimpy," he called.

There was a distant look in Gimp's eyes as he moved his head.

"Be careful, Tom. The condition he's in, he might bite you."

"Not now. Not even if he wanted to," Tom said.

I listened to the hurt in Tom's voice, "Come on, Gimpy. It can't end this way. We've been together too long, fellow." Then Tom turned to face me. "What can we do, Jim? We've got to do something," he said in an anxious voice.

"Gimpy, boy, "I called, trying to get some response.

"He heard you, Jim. He moved his head."

Tom's full attention stayed on Gimp, he didn't look at Al when he spoke to him. "What happened, Al?" he asked.

"I didn't know Gimp was around, and then all at once when I started backing up I heard a yelp."

"He was just over at the chapel site about thirty minutes ago," Tom said. "If only I'd stopped and taken time with him . . . . What're we going to do?" Tom asked again.

"The condition he's in, I'm not sure what we can do."

"You think he's going to die, don't you?"

"I didn't say that, Tom, but I don't know. You can see for yourself that he's hurt pretty badly."

"Gimpy, boy, we're going to do something for you," Tom said, gently placing his hand on him.

"I'll be back in a few minutes, Tom. I'm going over to supply to get a blanket and a couple of poles."

"Take it easy, old boy. You're my friend. It wouldn't be the same without you," I heard Tom say as I walked off. Then I heard Gimp whimper.

I was on my way out of supply, examining one of the poles and not paying much attention to where I was walking when I bumped into Robert.

"What's the hurry?" Robert asked when I looked up.

"It's Gimp. He's been hurt."

At first Robert didn't say anything. He appeared to be

stunned. Then he spoke. "Gimp! Where is he?" he asked excitedly.

"He's over next to the road, a good ways beyond where we're building the chapel. I just came over to get this blanket and a couple poles so that we can move him."

Robert was anxious to get to him. He took off running in front of me.

As I walked back over, I saw Tom still sitting next to Gimp. "Gimpy boy," I called, as I walked up to him hoping for a response. There was no movement, only lifelessness as he appeared to be near death.

"Take it easy, Gimpy," Robert said, getting down next to him.

"What do you think, Robert?" Tom asked.

Robert didn't say anything. He carefully placed his hand under Gimp's head and began to examine him.

"What do you think, Robert?" I asked as he stood up.

"I don't know if he'll make it through the night. He's hurt pretty badly."

"Do you think we can move him?" Tom asked.

"I don't know what it will do to him but we can't leave him out here," I replied.

"Gimpy, take it easy, fellow. It may hurt but we're going to move you," Tom said, speaking softly to him."

"Easy does it," I said as the three of us carefully slid the blanket under Gimp. Then with each side of the blanket rolled around the poles, Tom and I picked him up.

I looked at Gimp as we walked along and thought about what he meant not only to Tom but to all of us. In our loneliness as we went from one day to the next, Gimp was a companion, a source of strength that helped each of us along the way. He was always a jubilant dog, but there was no jubilance now.

"I'll get the door," Robert said as he took hold of the door knob.

"Gimp! What happened to him?" Duke asked as he stood up to look at him.

"He got hit by one of our trucks," Robert replied.

"It looks like it got him," Duke said as Gimp lay motionless.

We placed Gimp next to my bunk where I could listen and give him as much attention as possible.

"We just always took Gimp for granted," Duke remarked. "Just this afternoon I was petting him, not think ing much about him. Now we all know what he means to us."

"I just wish we could do something for him," Tom said.

"What about Arthur? He's the medic," Duke replied. "Maybe he could do something."

"You're right," Robert said. "I'll go find him. He's not a veterinarian but he's the next best that we have."

With the word out about Gimp's injury, it didn't take long for our hut to be filled with concerned G.I.'s. Observing Gimp lying motionless, they got down next to him and then with little response they got up and left.

"It took me a little time," Robert said, "but I found him."

I watched Arthur as he listened to the heart beat with his stethoscope and then as he took his hands and gently examined the rest of his body.

"What do you think, Arthur?" I asked as he stood up.

"I don't think he'll make it. He's hurt up on the inside."

"He's going to die, isn't he?" Tom asked.

"I believe so. From the way he's breathing, his diaphragm may have given way."

With all the concern for Gimp, it was 0100 hours before I finally got in bed. I knew as I lay awake unable to go to sleep that probably in a few hours he would be dead. Then suddenly I was awakened by Tom's voice.

"Jim, you awake?" Tom asked.

"Yeah," I replied as I awakened more fully.

"Look! Gimp's better. He's holding his head up."

"Are you sure?"

"Yeah, Look! See how he's holding it up?"

"You're right, Tom!" I replied as I watched Gimp lifting his head.

"Gimpy, you're going to live. I knew you would," Tom said, reaching over, touching him gently. "You made it through the night."

I pulled on my trousers as I watched Tom in all his anxiousness thinking that some way Gimp was going to pull through.

"You do think he'll live, don't you?" Tom asked.

"I don't know, Tom," I replied as I looked at Gimp with his head lifted and the rest of his body lying motionless.

"But he made it through the night."

"I know, but look at the rest of his body. He can't move."

"But there's hope. Even Arthur said he wouldn't make it through the night, but he did."

I was heading toward work as I looked in the direction where Gimp and the boys often played. It would be a long time, if ever, before they would see him again.

Throughout the day I continued to think about Gimp. At lunch time when I went by to check on him he was still about the same.

Later in the evening, with the day's work completed, I hurried back to the hut. I knew if there were any possibility for Gimp to live we would soon have to get some water down him. "Gimpy boy," I called as I watched the movement of his head. Seeing that he was still about the same, I took my canteen and went to the wash house and filled it with water. By the time I got back to the hut Tom was already there. In an effort to get the water down him, Tom held his head up while I placed the opening of the canteen into his mouth and gently stroked his throat. Tom smiled happily when he took the first few swallows. Then for the next several minutes I continued to hold the canteen and stroke his throat. Finally, with maybe one fourth of a cup of water in him, I left Tom and went on toward the chapel site. Shane and some of the others were working when I walked up.

"We stopped by your hut to see Gimp," Shane said.

"What do you think about him?" I asked.

"I don't know. He moved his head, but that was all. Still it surprises me that he made it through the night."

"I'm afraid it's his back. I'm afraid it's broken."

"You mean because he doesn't move the rest of his body?"

"Yeah. That's what I think."

"Where's Tom?" Gary asked.

"He's over at the hut with Gimp. He won't give up, not until Gimp is dead."

"Tom's a loner, Jim. Other than the chapel, Gimp and the boys are his life."

"I wish Tom would open up so that we could know him better," Shane said.

"He's always at mail call but I've never seen him get a letter," Gary responded as his mattock came downward making a popping, clanging sound when it struck against a rock.

I watched the puffy, frowning expression on Gary's face as he flung the mattock against the ground and started shaking his hands. "You swung it a little too hard," Shane said as he reached down and picked up the mattock. "Look at this split in the handle. That's why it hurt your hands."

"I didn't swing it too hard. It's just these . . . . I want say it," Gary replied shaking his head and holding out his hands so that we could see the redness in the palms.

Gary started to walk off, like he was going to leave. Then he stopped and turned and just looked. I assumed that it was the pain and then the frustrations that caused him to momentarily forget that he was on the mountain, and then when he started to walk off he realized there was really no better place to go.

"All that help, wonder where they are?" Gary asked as he walked back and picked up the mattock.

"Yeah, Shane, where's all that help you were talking about?" Henry asked with a snickering smile.

"I don't know, Henry, but you ought to be thankful anyway. Not everybody has the opportunity to get this kind of exercise."

"Pick up the shovel and get to work. You're not the cheering squad," Henry replied.

"I might not be the cheering squad but I'm the boss and you're the worker," Shane said as they were taking stabs at each other.

"Sure is important that you keep that brain working, Shane," Gary said, "or this would be such a dull place."

The work for the evening was nearing completion as I listened and occasionally threw in a punch. Then I walked over to the corner where Tom and I had discussed the cornerstone.

"Come on, Jim. Let's go in. It's time to call it a day," Gary said as they started to walk off.

"What are you looking at?" Shane asked, as he started walking toward me.

"I was talking with Tom about a cornerstone. What would you all think about one that possibly we could enclose a Bible and a small American flag in?"

"A cornerstone?" Gary replied.

"Yeah, one that we could enclose a Bible and a small American flag in, and when it's finished the date we started the chapel could be engraved on it."

"That sounds like a good idea," Shane replied.

"I like the idea of the Bible and the flag being enclosed," Gary commented with no apparent thought of his earlier frustrations.

We were walking along and still talking about the

---

chapel when Shane stopped and looked back. "You know it's a long way to go," he said, "but I can picture it. If it's ever finished, the way we've got it planned, it'll be beautiful, standing as a monument for God built by a lonely group of G.I.'s." We talked a little longer and then left.

"Gimpy boy," I called as I walked into the hut, and reached down to stroke his fur.

"What do you think?" Shane asked.

"He doesn't appear to be much better and he still hasn't drunk much water or eaten anything."

"Let me help you. We'll have to get some more water in him," Shane said, "or otherwise he'll surely die."

With a little effort we got him to take some water. An hour or so later I was alone with Gimp. He was lying quietly, not appearing to be in any pain. "Tom's got faith, fellow, and maybe, just maybe you'll make it. One thing about it, old boy, we won't give up, not as long as there's a breath of life in you. We'll keep trying. Listen, Gimpy, maybe that's Tom."

"Ted! I wasn't expecting you."

"I was down at the club talking with Gary. He said you all were talking about a cornerstone for the chapel."

"Yeah, we were talking about it. We thought we might put one in if it doesn't slow us down too much."

"That's what he mentioned. I wanted to let you know I'd be glad to carve the stone. That was my line of work before joining the army."

"I didn't know that, Ted. You never mentioned it before."

"It wasn't really the kind of work I cared for, so I never talked about it."

"But you were a stone mason?"

"Yeah, and if I had known I was going to be here I'd probably still be one. When Gary mentioned the cornerstone, it caught my attention. To be honest about it, Jim, I haven't given the chapel much thought until now. But you know, we all need the chapel."

"It's not going to be easy, Ted, but some way we'll get it built."

"It sounds like you've got company," Ted said, hearing a knock at the door.

"It's Tom. I'd know his knock anytime."

"Gimp any better?" Tom asked as he came in.

"Maybe about the same. Shane and I managed to get a little water in him."

A few minutes later I looked over at Ted as he was about to leave. "You going to be over at the chapel site tomorrow evening?" he asked.

"Yeah. We've still got a little more digging to do on the foundation," I replied as I listened to the seriousness of his voice.

"I thought if you all were going to be there, I'd come over and see how things are going."

"Just come on over. Come rain or shine we'll be there. We'll be looking for you."

I saw the surprised look on Tom's face as Ted was leaving.

"Did I hear Ted correctly or am I dreaming?" he asked.

"You're not dreaming, Tom. Ted said he'd like to cut the cornerstone for us. He was a stone mason before coming in the army."

"Cut the cornerstone, after all he said!" Tom remarked.

"Yeah. He said he was a stone mason in civilian life and that he'd like to help."

"Then that means we can put the cornerstone in?"

"Probably so." Ted seemed anxious to help us.

"That's really a surprise, isn't it?" Tom said as he turned his attention to Gimp. "And you say Gimp did take some more water?"

"Yeah, he took almost a glass full."

"You remember this morning he was holding his head

up, but this evening when I came by he was just lying there hardly moving." Tom said.

"We still had to raise his head, Tom, and then slowly work the water down his throat."

"But you do think he's doing better, don't you?"

"I'm not sure, Tom. It's just too early to tell."

"You hear that? Sounds like the rain is really coming down," Tom said as he looked up at the waving motion of the canvas.

Soon the wind started howling and the noise from the pounding rain and rapid movement of the canvas sounded loudly. Tom lay down on the floor beside Gimp and I stretched out on my bunk, lying flat on my back. Even though one of the huts was blown to pieces a few weeks earlier, there was nothing we could do but wait and hope. As I continued to watch the movement of the canvas I drifted into a twilight of sleep and then I began to dream that the walls of the chapel were going up. Later, I was surprised to awaken and find Tom sound asleep next to Gimp. I wasn't going to wake him but when I sat up on the side of the bunk Gimp responded to my movement by raising his head. With a surprised look, Tom sat up on the floor and reached his hand over and placed it on Gimp's head. At first we didn't say anything. Finally Tom said something about the boys.

"You seen them lately?" I asked.

"I saw them a few minutes this evening. After you left I stayed on with Gimp a little longer. Then I started to the chapel site but decided to go for a walk. The boys asked about Gimp. They wanted to know where he was."

"What did you tell them?"

"I didn't tell them anything. You know how much they like Gimp. I thought I'd wait a few days and see how he does."

Tom seemed lonely as I listened to him talking and watched the gentle movement of his hand on Gimp's body. Then I thought about what Shane said, "If only he could find a way to open up and talk." Maybe then, I thought, the hidden Tom would begin to surface. I wanted to ask him some personal questions but we were men and men don't ask personal questions. Soon the stormy weather was gone and calmness prevailed.

"Gimpy boy, you've got to get well," Tom said as he got up to leave.

The daylight hours were short, giving us little time to work each evening, but we never gave up. Ted meant what he said about the cornerstone. He seemed like a different person as he joined in, doing his part on the chapel. Far from making cutting remarks about the chapel, he was encouraging others to participate and he seemed pleased that he was drinking less.

Finally the digging was completed and Ted was still working on the stone and Gimp was still alive. It was Thursday afternoon and we were all lined up in the pay line. At first, when we were making the replica of the chapel, we were all enthusiastic, making plans and talking about how rapidly we would move forward. Then as I moved through the pay line and could see the replica of the chapel, I watched with an uncertainty, knowing that any real progress for the future depended on the contributions. Finally when the last person passed through the pay line, there was a lot of anticipation as we all gathered around to count the money. With all eyes looking, even including the captain, I lifted the top.

"What I was afraid of," Shane said, viewing the little amount of money.

"Fifty-three dollars," Gary said quietly as he watched the final count. "So what do we do now?" he asked.

"Just fifty-three dollars. Maybe you were right. Maybe we should have made it smaller," I replied.

"Don't be too disappointed," the captain said, giving us a word of encouragement. "You've got to remember where we are and that this is the first time."

"But it's just that we were hoping for more, Sir."

"I realize that, but for the first time you can't expect too much."

I waited, thinking the captain was going to say something else. Finally Ted responded, "We'll keep at it, Sir. It'll take time, but we'll get it built."

The captain turned and looked at me.

"Ted's speaking for all of us, Sir. We won't give up."

"That's what I wanted to hear. I don't know what the major has told you but he is very pleased with what you all are doing. Just the other day he and I were talking, watching you all as you were digging."

"We appreciate that, Sir, and we'll keep at it."

"See you fellows later," the captain said, picking up his briefcase.

"About the lumber for the foundation form, Jim, did we get enough money?" Henry asked.

"Only fifty-three dollars, Henry. You know that's not enough," Shane responded.

"But I was asking Jim, Shane."

"Like Shane said, Henry, it's probably not enough," I replied.

"And think of all the cement it's going to take," Gary remarked.

"And we're just talking about the lumber for the foundation form. Think about the cost of all the other material," Henry said. "Maybe like we talked about before, maybe we ought to make it smaller."

"But we ain't going to do that. I'm carving the cornerstone for the chapel like it's planned. Here, this won't help much but put it with the fifty three dollars," Ted said, handing me a five dollar bill.

"But you've already contributed, Ted," Gary said.

"Yeah, but not enough. Anyway I'd blow it at the club."

Ted's additional gift of five dollars started a chain reaction from the rest of us.

"Here's another five."

"And another five."

"And another five." Then with another five from me we had a total of seventy-eight dollars.

"Still not enough to get us started," Ted remarked.

"But you've given us the spark, Ted. Like you told the captain, some way we'll get it built."

"So what do we do now?" Henry asked.

"We'll figure out something," Shane replied.

"Some way we'll get it done. In the meantime this will give me more time to complete the cornerstone," Ted remarked.

"We'll do our part and let God do the rest," I said as I picked up the replica and started to leave.

"Look at what the chapel is already doing for us," I heard Ted say.

"But not all of us were like you," Bill said.

"I know," Ted replied. "For me it was one drink, then two, then three, then finally getting drunk practically every night." I listened to what Ted was saying, knowing that he desired to do differently. "I used to go to church, but it's been a long time," he said.

Maybe later on I'll talk with him about our Bible study, I thought as I walked off. "Gimpy, old boy," I said as I walked into the hut and placed the replica on the floor next to my bunk. "It's just you and me, the two of us, old fellow." Then quietly I sat down beside him and put my hand on his head. "You're getting better, but you've got to take it easy. It's going to take a long time. Here, Gimpy, this is just for you," I said, placing a piece of meat in his mouth. I watched Gimp with a painful look in his eyes, like he wanted to speak to me. I knew there was a better life for him. "You've got to get better, fellow. You've got to get back out on the mountain, out there with the children, Tom, and me. Life's not in here, not closed up under this canvas." I stood up and walked over to the replica. Reaching down, I removed the top. Such a little amount, I thought to myself as I raised my head and looked out the window. A few minutes later I reached over and picked up my Bible, the one Mom gave me, and started thumbing through the pages. I wasn't really looking for any particular scripture when I saw Mom's handwriting. I started reading, becoming somewhat emotional.

Remember Son,

Back home we are thinking of you daily. Each day we are praying for you. Make it your aim always to accept God as your source of help for your every need. God never fails us you know. Herein lies the peace that passes understanding. Leaning upon the strength of God, you will do your duties well, and you will be living the Good Life; herein realizing something of this deep peace that passes understanding.

Love,
Mom

With tears flowing, I paused for a moment. I closed my eyes and took time to talk with God. Then with my eyes opened and a renewed strength, I felt better. "Gimpy, old boy, I'll be back after awhile," I said as I walked toward the door. Moments later I stood outside, feeling the briskness of the air from the wind blowing in off the sea. My hair was tousling and it felt like springtime, back when the birds were singing and the fields were plowed and a newness of life was being born. I looked up as I walked toward the chapel site, taking time to view the beauty of a cloud. Watching its movement slowly shadowing the brightness of the moon, I thought about home. "Dad, it's still there. It'll always be there for us as long as we live." Then with the cloud drifting on and the brightness of the moon returning, I walked up to the chapel site. Viewing the piles of dirt and rocks, recalling something of the problems we experienced, I began to think about all of the difficulties that were ahead, from being in the military to being in a Moslem country, wondering if the chapel could ever be built. In a moment of meditation I bowed my head. *God, that Thy will be done through us, I pray.*

Then as I looked out into the twilight, I knew that somewhere on down the mountain, Tom was there. I looked upward and listened. The gentle breeze was bristling against my face and the soft sound of music was flowing through the air. I walked on for several minutes and then being a little careless, I stumbled. "Tom," I said as I walked up behind him. Tom quickly turned around.

"You frightened me. I wasn't expecting you," he said.

"I didn't mean to. I was out walking and heard you blowing the harmonica. I thought I'd come on down and talk with you."

"I guess you think I've lost interest in the chapel."

"Why do you say that?"

"Oh, I don't know. It's just that I haven't been over in the last few days."

"That's okay, Tom. We all need to be to ourselves once in awhile."

"About the money, how much did we get?"

"Not very much. There was only fifty-three dollars. Then Ted, Gary, Shane, Henry, and I each put in another five dollars."

I watched Tom as he reached for his pocketbook and handed me another five dollars.

"That makes eighty-three, Tom."

"It's still not enough to hardly get us started, is it?"

"Probably not, but we'll keep going."

"Now that we've dug the foundation, what can we do without more money?"

"I'm not sure. Ted said he'd finish the cornerstone and I've got to check on the price of materials."

"With the time we have left, it doesn't look very good, does it?"

"Not really but maybe if we keep at it, we'll get the material some way."

Tom started blowing the harmonica again and then he stopped and reached into the pocket of his field jacket. "What is it?" I asked as he extended his hand.

"It's a picture of Gimp."

"A picture of Gimp?"

"Yeah. One that I took in your hut. Mac developed it for me. I'm going to give it to Mehmet."

"You still haven't told them, have you?"

"Not yet. I thought I'd wait and give them the picture first."

. . . .

I stayed on with Tom awhile longer, thinking the boys would come. Finally I got up and went back up to the club.

"Jim, over here," I heard Ted call.

"Are you in?" Bill asked.

"Yeah, deal me in," I replied as I watched Bill dealing out the cards.

We played on for awhile. Unlike before, Ted seemed like a different person. He drank less and he made no reference to the coke I was drinking. Finally I decided to go in.

"It's pay day, Young'un, no time to quit," Bill said.

"I'm going in, Bill. I've got to get some sleep."

"But that's all you ever do," Bill replied, kidding me as he continued to deal out the cards.

"Seriously, Bill, I'm going in," I said as he started to deal me in.

"Jim, you going in?" Simms called.

"Yeah. I've got to get some sleep. You coming?"

"Not yet. I'll be on after awhile."

"Come on, Young'un, it's pay day. It's time to live it up."

"You fellows finish it up. I'm going in."

Knowing that Duvone was probably asleep, I tried to be quiet as I opened the door.

"That you, Jim?" Duvone asked as he turned over.

"Yeah. I didn't mean to wake you."

"You didn't. I just got in a few minutes ago."

"Is Duke in?" I asked as I slid my trousers down, trying to get in bed without turning the light on.

"Yeah. He came in at the same time I did. But don't worry, you won't wake him, not 'till morning."

"He's been waiting for this for a long time and now he's celebrating going home," I remarked.

"It's going to be our turn one of these days, but right now it still seems like a life-time away," Duvone replied as he turned over to go to sleep.

For two hours or more I lay in bed with my thoughts rambling as I watched the twinkling of the stars. Then the noise started. The commotion was coming in our direction. It was Simms and some of his buddies. I heard Mark speak.

"We got you here, Simms. This is your hut," Mark said.

"You sure this is my hut?" Simms asked.

"Simms, don't you know where you live," Chad muffled when the door opened and they all stumbled in.

"What's going on?" Duvone yelled as he awakened to the noise.

"We were having a party and they ran us out of the club." Chad's voice muffled again.

"Get up and join us. We brought the drinks," Mark's voice sounded.

"Go have your party somewhere else and take Simms with you and keep him," Duvone yelled.

Just as I stood up to turn the light on, I stumbled. It was Simms lying on the floor. "Jim," he called.

"Simms, why don't you and your cruds go jump in the sea?" Duvone yelled angrily as he stood up.

They were all drunk but they knew Duvone meant business. In a way it was funny—Simms lying on the floor and the rest of them stumbling, trying to help each other out the door.

As I looked at the helpless Simms, I was tempted to let him stay on the floor. "Jim," he called. "Help me up."

"I told you before, Simms, the bottle is going to get you if you keep on."

"It don't matter. Besides, nobody cares about any of us, you know that," Simms said as I helped him onto his bed.

"I tell you one thing, Simms, you and your buddies better be concerned. We're not going to keep putting up with this mess," Duvone yelled almost uncontrollably.

Duvone was so angry he couldn't go to sleep. Fifteen minutes later he was still mumbling while Duke was sleeping through it all.

Chapter 7

---◆---

With a total of eighty-three dollars in contributions and bad weather conditions, there was no longer the anxiousness that once prevailed. Still, we were striving for ways that would move us forward. I checked on the price of materials and got some good news. The gravel would be free and the sand would cost very little, but with our small amount of money we couldn't buy the necessary cement and lumber needed for pouring the foundation.

I was over at the chapel site talking with Henry and Shane. We were trying to decide what to do next.

"It seems like we're at a dead end," Shane said, when suddenly Henry looked in the direction of post engineers and then he turned back with a grin and said, "I've got an idea."

"You and your brain, it couldn't be much," Shane replied, his hazel blue eyes sparkling.

"What is it, Henry?" I asked.

"The eighty-three dollars we've got would buy enough cement to get us started on the foundation . . . ."

Henry didn't finish before Shane interrupted. "But first

---◆---

we would have to buy the lumber to build the foundation forms," Shane remarked. "So what's your idea?"

"You didn't let me finish, Shane. With all the lumber post engineers have, maybe we could borrow enough from them and then replace it later."

Shane raised his right hand and rubbed his forehead as his little grin tightened to a firmness. "Henry's got an idea, Jim. What do you think? Do you think post engineers would let us have the lumber?"

"I'm not sure, but it would be worth a try."

"But why wouldn't they?" Henry asked.

"We're in the army, Henry and you know what that means," Shane replied.

Henry and I understood what Shane was saying. We knew that even though the major was supporting us, with a rank less than E-5 we had to answer to the N.C.O.'s and we knew very well that only post engineers were supposed to do the building. Still, Henry's suggestion was a good one. After a little more discussion, it was decided that I would check with post engineers to see if they would loan us enough lumber to build the foundation forms. With renewed enthusiasm, I walked to my hut. As I opened the door and walked in, Tom looked up at me and spoke.

"Look at Gimp, Jim. See how hard he's trying to get up, but he can't stand on his hind legs."

"I know, Tom. I've been watching him."

For the next few minutes I sat on my bunk and watched the tiring efforts of Gimp, using his front legs, trying to walk as Tom lifted his hindquarters. Several times Tom reached down and picked Gimp up, and then each time as he slowly released his support, Gimp's hindquarters slumped to the floor. With some concern about Gimp's back, I kept watching Tom's determination.

"He can't walk," Tom finally conceded in a faint, wavering voice.

One more time, Gimp seemed to be saying as he turned his head in expectation.

"You're going to be okay," Tom said as he lay down beside him and placed his arm around him.

"I'm going over to post engineers, Tom. I'll be back before long," I said as I walked off.

It took only a few minutes and I could see the lumber. As I got closer I stopped and looked. Maybe Henry was right, maybe we could get the lumber, I thought. There were at least three new loads hauled in. Soon I was standing at the door anticipating what to say. As I opened the door and stepped inside, I quickly realized that I was being ignored. I waited, expecting someone to speak to me, and then I took another few steps forward. Feeling the tension I finally spoke. "Sergeant Dooley," I said, calling his name. I waited and when he didn't answer, I turned and started out.

"Were you speaking to me?" he asked in a commanding voice as I was about to open the door.

"Yes, Sir," I answered, somewhat nervous, as I turned around and took a few steps toward him.

"Is there something we can do for you?"

"We were wondering if we might be able to borrow some lumber from you?"

"Lumber! What do you need lumber for?"

"The chapel, Sir. I don't know whether you're aware of it or not but we're trying to build one."

"Yeah, I'm aware of it," Sergeant Dooley responded with his piercing eyes saying more than his words.

"It's the chapel we wanted to borrow it for. You probably saw the replica set up in the pay line for contributions."

"So that was for contributions?"

"Yes, Sir, but we didn't get very much. We didn't get enough to get us started. We were wondering if we might be able to borrow enough lumber for the foundation forms and then later when our contributions are enough we'll buy more lumber and return it."

I waited, watching Sergeant Dooley's expression becoming more relaxed as he spoke. "I wish we could help you," he said, "but we've got to use the lumber for other purposes. You understand, don't you?"

"Yes, Sir. Thanks anyway."

With a let down feeling but not totally surprised, I turned and walked back to my hut. Henry and Shane were waiting for me.

"It was bad news, wasn't it?" Shane asked as I opened the door and walked in.

"Yeah. It was bad news."

"What did he say, Jim?" Henry asked.

"He said they needed the lumber for other purposes."

"Other purposes! That doesn't surprise me," Shane replied.

"What do you mean?" Henry asked.

"It's simple, Henry. They're post engineers. We're not supposed to know anything about building. Besides we're just peons. It's just that simple."

With only eighty-three dollars and no idea of how we could move forward we brainstormed for awhile and then Shane and Henry left. I looked at the picture of Mom and Dad and then I sat on the floor next to Gimp.

"Gimpy boy," I said as I reached over to place my hand on his head. Then suddenly he tried desperately to get up. "Easy fellow, take it easy boy," I said, calming him down as I stroked his fur with a gentle touch.

"Careful, Jim," Duke said as I tried to help Gimp to his feet.

"It's no use. He can't walk, Duke."

"Like I mentioned before, I think it's his back. He may never be able to walk again," Duke replied.

"But he's come a long way. You saw him trying to get up just a moment ago."

"I know and that's not good, not the way he was trying to get up," Duke said as he came over to examine him.

I watched, listening to Gimp whimper as Duke took hold of him. "It is his back, isn't it?"

"I believe so and his leg is messed up pretty badly too."

"Maybe if we put a splint on the leg, that'd help to keep him down a while longer. What do you think?"

"It wouldn't hurt. Look at this. I didn't realize it was this bad," Duke said, showing me his leg.

It took at least thirty minutes to get the splint fixed in a stable position. First I removed a board from my home-made desk while Duke was making a roping material by ripping up one of his old towels. Then Gimp started whining as we moved his leg to get the board into a secured position. Finally we had the splint on and Gimp was lying next to my bunk. I continued to watch him for a few minutes and then decided to go for a walk.

"It's mighty dark out there," Duke said as I opened the door.

I walked along in the darkness of night, being able to see only the twinkling of the stars as I carefully guided my footsteps along the way. On toward the dug foundation I slowly moved when quickly I jumped at the sound of Ted's voice.

"Young'un, is that you?" Ted asked.

At first I didn't answer. Ted spoke again.

"Young'un, is that you?" he called in a louder voice.

"Yeah, Ted. It's me. I'm over here."

"Take it easy. It's dark out here. I fell a few minutes ago," Ted cautioned.

"What brings you out here?" I asked.

"I was talking with Shane. He told me about you going to post engineers."

"Yeah. I tried to borrow enough lumber for the foundation forms."

"That's what he said. He said they wouldn't let you have it."

"That's right. Sergeant Dooley said they needed it for other purposes."

"Sergeant Dooley! That doesn't surprise me."

"It wouldn't make any difference who it was, Ted. Like Shane said, the way we've planned the chapel, nobody believes it can be built, not even us sometimes. Just look at the size of it and the time we have left."

"Are you saying we're quitting?"

"No, I'm not saying that."

"So what are you saying?"

"I'm not sure. Do you have any ideas?"

"Ideas?" Ted asked. "I think we've run out of ideas.

"But that's not what you told the captain."

"And I'm not saying we're quitting either."

"So what are you saying, Ted?"

"I'm not sure. It seems like we're all confused."

"Maybe like Shane and Gary said, maybe we should have made it smaller," I replied.

"But no longer than we've been at it, we haven't given it a fair chance. If we stay with it, someday it'll be finished."

"You really believe that, don't you, Ted?"

"Yes, I do. You see what the chapel has already done for me, don't you? I used to go to church and read my Bible. Now for the last few weeks I've started back again."

I understood what Ted was saying and it was encouraging. Still, with only fifty-three dollars contributed in the pay line, there were doubts.

"When everyone sees the foundation going in, it'll be different," Ted said.

"I hope so."

"It will be. Take my word for it. You can see what it's done for me."

"I know what you're saying, Ted, but it's going to take a long time, much longer than we have."

"But we're not the only ones. Others will come after us."

God speaks to us in a lot of ways, I thought. Just now he spoke to me through Ted. "We won't give up, Ted. Someday the chapel will stand as a monument to God. It will be a testimony of God's word lifting one G.I. up to the other."

"A couple of more days and I'll have the cornerstone finished," Ted said.

In the moments that followed, Ted and I sat in the darkness of the night, uplifted by the presence of God, hearing only the faint sounds from the roaring of the sea. Then I began to see a little redness across the horizon. "The moon is coming up, Jim. Look at all the redness. It's pretty, isn't it?" Ted remarked.

"It never changes, Ted. It will always be the same. It's always there for us. It reminds me of being back home. Back when I was growing up and I used to go out at night and look up at the moon and the stars. Sometimes I would be overwhelmed by the mere thought that I'm so small and yet I live, I'm able to look up into the heavens above and comprehend something of the greatness of it all."

"I know," Ted replied. "And it reminds me of home too. In forty-three more days I'll be leaving. I'll get home in time for Christmas. How about you, Young'un? How much longer do you have."

"I still have a long time, Ted, almost five months."

"But it'll go by. I always watched the other fellows leaving, knowing that they came like I did."

A little later I walked down to the club with Ted. As we walked in there was a call for quiet. George was going to give a speech.

"Come on, George. You've got the floor," Bill said, sitting a couple tables over.

"Okay fellows, okay," George responded, having some difficulty standing up.

"Speech, George, speech," two or three shouted.

I watched George, the big smile on his face, knowing that it was his night, the night he spent twelve months for.

"Come on, George, you can make it," came the words of encouragement as he stood up.

With a big grin on George's face, he started to speak. "I've been waiting a long time for this. You fellows are not going to be seeing me around much longer. This is my last night so drink up, it's all on me."

Then I watched George with the big smile disappearing as he sat down.

"Come on, Young'un, this one's for George," Bill said placing the bottle in front of me.

"That's it, Young'un. You're growing up now," Robert said, apparently thinking I was going to take a drink.

Soon the game was underway and no one paid me any attention when I ignored the drink. It was just a routine night and everything was going as usual when I looked across the room and saw Chad stumble and fall to the floor. No one paid him much attention as he lay on the floor and they continued the game without him. A few minutes later I was holding a full house, three nines and two queens, when Tom rushed in and called my name.

"What is it?" I asked as I turned around.

"It's Gimp, something's wrong with him!" Tom said anxiously.

"Young'un, this is George's night. You not leaving, are you?" Bill asked.

"Yeah, I've got to see about Gimp, " I replied as I looked at George hardly knowing what was going on.

Tom and I moved quickly toward the hut.

"He's in a lot of pain," Tom said. "Just as I was walking up to your hut I could hear him. Then when I opened the door I could see him. He was next to Simms' bunk and there was blood coming from his hind leg."

"Gimp's still in bad shape, Tom. Now that he's trying to get up, it puts him in a lot of pain."

"But the way he's trying, he's bound to be much better."

"Yeah, he seems to be better but some way we're going

to need to keep him down, give his back and leg more of a chance to heal."

"But he needs exercise, doesn't he?"

"Probably some, but for the time being, with all the pain he has and the way his back and leg are, I think we need to keep him lying down as much as possible."

"But the way he's trying to move, how we going to do that?"

"We'll need to fix a better splint across his back and down his leg."

"But how do you know that's the right thing to do?"

"The way his back and leg are, it just makes good sense."

When we walked in Gimp was lying next to my bunk and Duke was sitting beside him. "How is he, Duke?" I asked.

"He seems to be doing okay now."

"But when I came in a little earlier, you ought to have seen him," Tom said. "He was lying on his other side bleeding with his leg folded under him."

"I just moved him over here and then wiped the blood up," Duke said.

Duke, Tom and I decided to fix a new splint, one that we thought would keep him down. When the splint was finished I sat down on my bunk and looked at Gimp with his head lifted and his eyes facing Tom. "Here, Gimpy," Tom said, reaching down, giving him a piece of meat.

It was late the next evening when someone hollered mail call. A short time later Tom and I were standing next to each other, waiting to hear the names called.

"No use in your being here, Young'un," Robert said as he walked up behind me.

"Speak for yourself, Robert. I'm going to get all kinds of mail," I said with a smile.

"As ugly as you are, I'd hate to see the looks of the girl that's writing you."

"That's all a matter of opinion," I replied, knowing he was unaware that I had no girl friend.

Soon everyone gathered around and the wooden shutters opened.

Beginning to think I wasn't going to get a letter, I got all excited when I heard the name Boyte called. Reaching out, taking the letter in my hand, I felt the closeness and warmth of home. Then I continued to listen and watch, knowing that soon the shutters would close and some would walk away empty handed. Finally the shutters closed.

"I see you got a letter," Robert said.

"Yeah," I replied, knowing that he didn't get one.

I walked off at a distance. Then recalling Tom standing beside me, I suddenly turned around trying to see where he was. Being unable to see him, I opened my letter and began to read:

Dear Son,

We hope you are doing fine and so much want to hear from you more often. Your dad is always watching the mail and keeps saying maybe we'll get a letter from Jim Boy today. It's just that we're always anxious to know how you are doing.

As for all of us, we're doing okay. John was in last weekend and we're all so anxious, knowing that soon Joe will be home, and then another few months you'll be coming home . . . .

With feelings of regret, knowing I needed to write more often, I finished reading Mom's letter.

"You better head in, Jim, it's beginning to rain," Shane called.

I was headed toward the chapel site, but with the rain beginning to come down harder and the wind blowing I turned around and picked up my pace, running as I headed toward the hut.

"It's coming down, isn't it?" Duke said as I opened the door.

"Yeah, all at once the bottom fell out," I replied as I closed the door. I watched Gimp's quick movement, appearing to be somewhat nervous as he responded to the rapid movement of the canvas. Hearing the pounding of the rain against the canvas, I walked over and sat down on my bunk. I was still holding the letter in my hand, feeling the closeness of home, when I looked over, seeing a different Simms. He was sitting in loneliness with his head bowed, holding his letter. Then moments later when he raised his head, I knew something was wrong. He was clutching his letter and deep within his bloodshot eyes was the pain of hurt as tears began to come.

"I see you got a letter, Simms," I said, making conversation.

"Finally," he replied, speaking softly.

I waited, watching as he reached into his footlocker. "Did I ever show you the pictures of my children?"

"I don't think so."

"This one is John, he's my oldest, and this one is Sammy, next to the oldest, and this one, this is my little Susie. They're my children. They're all I've got to live for," he said, speaking in a quivering voice.

I knew Simms was hurting and he needed someone to talk to.

"You've got a good looking family, Simms," I said as I watched the tears flooding his eyes.

"The letter I got, I should've known."

In the dreariness of all the rain and blowing wind, I felt only coldness as I sat waiting, wondering what it was that Simms started to tell me. "Simms," I started to say and then he spoke.

"The chapel, Jim, how's it coming?"

"I'm not sure. It seems that we're having a lot of difficulty in getting started."

"That's what Ted was telling us. He said he wondered if you were about ready to give up."

"Sometimes I feel like it but it's not just me building the chapel. There're several of us and we're not going to give up."

"We need the chapel, Jim. We all need it. Who knows, sometime in the future after we're long gone, they might even have a full time chaplain here."

I knew from past conversation that Simms loved his family. Now he felt the need for a chaplain, the need for someone to talk to.

"Look at that, would you. The wind's getting mighty strong," Duke said.

"The way it started, it came up all at once," I replied as I began to wonder how much longer the canvas would hold up against the powerful force of the wind.

"If it's like all the others, the storm will blow over before long," Duke said as we all calmly sat watching the motion of the canvas.

"That's it," Simms said when the lights stopped blinking and we were left in total darkness.

"It's okay, Gimpy. We're going to make it," I said, placing my hand on his head.

Then later, when the storm was over, I stood up in the darkness and felt my way to the door.

"That you, Jim?" Duke asked as I opened the door.

"Yeah," I replied, feeling the coolness of the air, being over taken by the calmness that prevailed.

"It's gone, isn't it?" Duke asked.

"Yeah, you were right. The storm moved on." Then as I listened to the crashing waves, I thought about our mission and about the Soviet Union, wondering how long it would be before it too would be silenced like the death waiting for the raging storm on the sea.

Chapter 8

It seemed that all of our efforts were failing, leaving us with little hope. Yet we continued to talk and to pray, hoping that some way we could get started.

Shane and I were talking, exchanging some thoughts about the cornerstone, when Ted walked up.

"Where've you guys been?" Ted asked.

"Up here waiting to go home," Shane replied, smiling.

"You find the way off, let me know and I'll go with you," Ted replied.

With a more serious thought, the smile on Ted's face was gone. "There's something I've been thinking about, Jim."

"What's on your mind," I asked, observing his seriousness.

"I was lying awake last night thinking. What would you think of our going ahead and borrowing the lumber?"

"You mean take it without asking?" Shane asked with a big grin.

"Not exactly, Shane. Part of the problem is that Jim has already asked."

"That's right, but we could still take it," Shane said, looking over toward me with the grin no longer there.

"It was just a thought, maybe a way we could get started."

I listened to what Ted said, knowing I'd been thinking the same thing.

"What do you think, Jim?" Shane asked.

"It looks like it's our only choice. Some way we've got to get the foundation in. Like Duke said, we've got to let everyone know that we're serious about building the chapel."

"But just as soon as we take it, Young'un, Sergeant Dooley's going to be right on you and you know what that means."

"I realize what you are saying, Ted, but I still think it might be our only choice."

"And there's something else to think about, it could be the end of the chapel if we do it."

"It's the end anyway, Ted, unless we get something started."

"Yeah, it seems like it's been the end from the beginning. But once we get the lumber maybe it'll be different. Besides, Sergeant Dooley won't do anything, the old man is behind us," Shane said.

"That's good thinking, Shane, except for one thing."

"What's that, Ted?"

"You've got to remember that we're still in the army."

"But you're doing double talk, Ted. A few minutes ago you were suggesting we take the lumber and now . . ."

"I'm not saying we don't take it. It's just that we've got to be careful and take a little time, use the old brain, you know. That's all I'm saying."

I listened to what was being said, trying to reason in my mind the taking of the lumber for the chapel.

"What about it, Jim? What're we going to do?" Shane asked, verbalizing his excitement.

"I'm not sure, Shane. Maybe like I said, maybe it's all we can do," I replied, watching the bubbling excitement in Shane's eyes.

"That's the way I see it if we expect to get anything done."

"But it's the Young'un's neck, Shane. He's already asked for the lumber."

"Maybe if we take a couple of days and think it through," I replied.

"And listen, we want to keep it quiet. We can't afford to talk about it too much," Ted said.

"But what about the rest? We're going to let them know, aren't we?" Shane asked.

"Yeah, if we decide to do it. We're all building the chapel and whatever we do, we'll do it together."

"I can just see Sergeant Dooley. He's got the mind of the army but we've got the brains," Shane said bouncing around and slapping me on the shoulder.

"Just remember, Shane, we're all part of the army and we've got to be careful."

"Just six more months," Shane replied and then he quietly mumbled, "Only problem it's still a lifetime away."

The mood became solemn and all was silent, Ted was looking down toward the sea. "Would you all like to go see the cornerstone?" he asked.

"Sounds good to me," Shane replied as soon the three of us were strolling along. We were about half way down the mountain when Shane spotted Tom and the boys. We stopped to watch their joyful play for a few minutes and then Shane started whistling as we walked on toward them.

Mehmet got all excited and almost stumbled as he started toward me. "Em," he called with his black wavy hair tousling in the wind and his little boyish brown eyes beaming with a happy smile.

"*Merhaba*," I replied, telling him hello as I reached over and patted him on the head.

"Gimp!" he said as his broad smile faded and he handed me a picture.

"*Evet,*" I replied, saying yes, letting him know that I understood as I took the picture in my hand.

"Is that a picture of Gimp?" Ted asked.

"Yeah, Tom made it for the boys."

"Gimp," Mehmet said again with his little smile overshadowed by a grim look as I handed the picture back.

"Yes, it's Gimp," I replied, as I watched his deep compassion, clutching the picture firmly in his hand. I looked over at Tom, observing his pleasant smile, knowing that he was pleased with Mehmet's response to the picture.

"He likes the picture," Tom said.

"Yeah, I can see that he does."

"Gimp better?" Taner asked.

"Yeah, Gimp's better."

I watched Mehmet as he reached the other hand in his pocket. "Gimp," He said, handing me a little piece of meat.

"He's all concerned about Gimp, isn't he?" Ted asked.

"Yeah, Gimp means a lot to him," I replied as I watched the tender smile on his face, knowing he wanted me to feed it to Gimp.

"You guys just out walking?" Tom asked.

"We were on our way to look at the cornerstone. Would you like to come along?"

"I might as well, it's about time for the boys to go in."

"*Gel, gel,*" Tom called, telling the boys to come on as we began to walk down the mountain. Then Tom turned to me and mentioned the sand.

"Sand! I take care of it," Taner said, speaking excitedly.

"Is this the boy you were talking about?" Ted asked.

"Yeah, this is Taner. He's the one that located the sand for us. He can speak some English."

"I work with you," Taner replied, obviously pleased that he located the sand.

As we walked along, Mehmet kept clutching the picture, struggling at times to stay at Tom's side. Finally, as we were nearing the bottom of the mountain, the boys waved and said good-bye, then turned and slowly walked off.

"You coming, Jim?" Shane called as I slowed the pace for Tom to catch up.

"Is the Young'un too slow for you, Shane?" Ted asked.

"Yeah, he's been in the army too long. He gets any slower we'll have to carry him."

"It sounds like you've got the mind of a career soldier, Young'un," Ted smarted as he turned to Shane and winked. Then it was laughter, first by Ted and Shane, then by all four of us. The mere thought of being a career soldier was so farfetched.

"Not yet, Ted," I replied. "That won't happen to me. You fellows may be career soldiers but not me. I'm going to be fast enough to find my way out of the army."

"But you've got to get off the mountain first, Young'un."

Ted's remark was final. I didn't respond and the joking ended.

When Ted took on the project of cutting the cornerstone he made a suggestive comment that he would rather we not come down until he finished it. I knew that we must be getting closer to the stone, Ted's walk was becoming faster. "Down this way," he said as we finally turned to go down one of the old ox cart roads.

"Couldn't you pick a better place than this?" Tom asked, observing the deepness of the ruts, trodden down by the passage of ox carts over a long period of time.

Being anxious to see the cornerstone, I was looking further down the road when I slipped and almost fell.

"Careful, Young'un," Ted said, as he caught me by the arm.

"Now I understand what you meant by your brain out-doing your legs," Shane remarked, his voice sounding with laughter.

No quicker had Shane spoken than he slipped in the mud and fell in some water. It wasn't really funny, but all the mud and being wet, the sight was just too much for us not to laugh.

"So the joke's on me," Shane said, his quickness of thought turning to a grin. "How much further?" he asked, obviously feeling wet and cold.

"We're almost there," Ted replied with a sound of anxiousness in his voice as each footstep drew us nearer. As we got closer, I knew this was an exciting moment for Ted—the moment he had been waiting for, the moment to show us the cornerstone.

"There it is," Ted said, speaking proudly as he pointed to it.

At first I didn't say anything. I was amazed at the quality of work as I walked around it. Then I got down next to the stone. There I saw the perfection of work as I felt its smoothness and examined the hole where the Bible and the American flag were to be housed. Being surprised by the high quality of work, I turned to Ted, "I thought you said you weren't a professional, Ted. It couldn't have been done better. You did a superb job."

"I'm not a professional, Young'un. Doing stone work was just a job."

"Maybe so but you've done a heck of a job on this one, and look, it's almost completed."

"I would have completed it earlier but it's so far out here to walk, and then with such a few hours to work on it. You know how that is."

"Yeah, I know how that is but it's top quality. You couldn't have done better," I replied as I watched Tom and Shane examining the stone.

"God's word and the great American flag and our memories will be kept here," Shane remarked, placing his hand in the hole.

"May be that we leave none of our names in the stone, only our memories, with our names written in the Good Book," Ted said.

Just to see the stone and to know that God was with us was a great moment. We stayed on a little longer and then left. As we walked along going back up the mountain, I could sense from our conversation that finally the building of the chapel was underway.

Back on the mountain, I opened the door to my hut and with no one around, I walked over and sat down beside Gimp. I placed my hand on him and gently began to rub him. Then as I watched his efforts trying to get up, I wondered if he would ever be able to walk again. "Gimpy, old boy," I said, "I've got something for you. You remember the little boys, don't you? Well, they haven't forgotten you and they never will. It's just that they can't come up here. They aren't allowed to." I reached in my pocket and pulled out the little piece of meat. "Here, Gimpy," I said. "Little Mehmet sent this to you. He wanted you to have something from him. And something else, Gimpy, Tom knows that I'm taking care of you, but he's the one that held out. He never gave up from the very beginning and he needs you. He's a lonely G.I. in need of a friend."

I was still talking to Gimp when Gary knocked and then opened the door. From the expression on his face, I knew there must be something important. "What's up?" I asked.

"I was just down at the club talking with Shane and Ted. They said we might go ahead and take the lumber from post engineers."

"That's what we're thinking about, Gary," I replied as I watched the grinning smile, knowing that he was hoping and anticipating some excitement coming from it all.

Then Gary's expression changed and there was a firmness in his voice as he spoke somewhat despondent. "But after we get the lumber, Jim, they'll know that we took it."

"That may be, but we haven't got any other choice, Gary, not if we expect to get something done on the chapel.

"So we're really going to take it, that's what you're saying, isn't it?"

"That's my thinking, if everyone is in agreement. I just don't see any other way around it."

Gary's eyes immediately lit up and a brightness shone on his face. "You hear that, Gimpy? Old Sergeant Dooley is not going to outdo us. We're in for some excitement, old boy. You need to get up and get out there with us," Gary said as he reached down and rubbed Gimp's fur.

Just like Shane, Gary's mind was rampaging and his pulse was running rapid as he sat down on Simms's bunk. But the excitement of it all was too much. He quickly got up and left. Then I reached over and picked up my Bible and read a portion of the scripture and then bowed my head.

> God, I pray that as we move forward in the building of the chapel, that Your will and Your will alone guide and direct us, that we don't let the excitement of the moment lift us out of Your reach.

Then putting the Bible back in its place, I sat staring at the picture of Mom and Dad. *Dad, we never had much to work with. It just seemed that it was always intended to be that way for us. And now we're over here trying to build a chapel and just like always before, we don't have much to work with but those words that you spoke so many times, "If we just keep at it we can do it." That's what we're doing and we know that someday the chapel will stand high on this mountain, symbolizing the efforts of man to come closer to God.*

Then with my thoughts turning to Gimp, I walked over to him. "Gimpy, old boy, life's not always easy, not for any of us, but you're going to make it," I said, reaching down stroking his fur. With Gimp's head raised, his eyes focused, hearing only the faint sounds from the crashing of the waves in the sea, he watched, unable to get up as I turned to leave. I slowly walked to the mountainside and sat on the ground.

There I listened to the softness of the music flowing through the air, knowing that its cry of loneliness was reaching out. Through the hour I sat, being fully engrossed, totally absorbed by the realms of beauty that were driving inwardly, magnifying feelings, making them reach to heights unknown. Losing track of time, I sat on into the evening. Then finally I got up and slowly journeyed back up the mountain. At first I had thoughts of turning in but I saw the lights at the club and decided to stop by.

"You fellows still at it?" I asked as I walked up to the table where Ted, Henry, Shane, and Gary were sitting.

"Young'un!" Ted spoke. "We were about to think you weren't coming down."

"The Young'un's growing up, Ted. He's getting slow in his old age," Bill said.

"But I'm still young enough that I can stand up," I responded, maybe throwing the punch a little low.

"You trying to say I'm drunk, Young'un?"

"I didn't say that, Bill. Whatever gave you an idea like that?"

"I don't know. Maybe it's because I am drunk. You think I am?"

"Maybe a little."

"Okay, so I'm drunk. Get a coke. It's on me."

"Thanks, Bill," I replied, taking a seat.

With the card game in progress, I welcomed and desired the closeness that existed among all of us.

"What's this about the lumber?" Henry asked.

"Gary told you, didn't he? We're going to take it if everybody is in agreement." Ted stopped and held the cards firmly and Shane gave a thumbs up.

"We're all ready. Let's get on with it," Gary remarked loudly.

"Quiet! Not so loud, Gary," Ted said, calming him down.

"Sorry about that. I almost forgot," Gary said, obviously being overtaken by the thought of doing something different, doing something exciting on the mountain and finally, most of all, moving ahead with building the chapel. Ted put the cards in his pocket and we moved to a table further over where we could talk and not be heard. For further planning we met the next evening at 1900 hours in the mess hall.

We were in the military and we knew the importance of planning. To try to ensure there were no mistakes, we started our plan by first considering all the strategic locations. Then we traced all of the movements from beginning to the end. In conclusion we decided it must be a pitch black night, not even a star shinning. To ensure confidentiality and a method by which we could have roll call, a number was assigned to each person, and then so that no one saw us as a group, we were to leave our huts separately and meet at a point about two hundred feet below the E.M. Club. From there we were to move down the mountain and then come up on the back side by security location.

With the plans completed, we waited with confidence for the perfect night. Several nights passed, still there were only scattered clouds. Anxiety was building. Finally it was the perfect night—a total overcast. Yet it was so pitch black as I left my hut that I began to wonder if we could pull it off; were our decisions the right ones. I walked on by the club. Only fifty more steps to go and still not a sound from anyone. I was down to thirty-five steps.

"Number one, is that you?" a voice sounded.

"Yeah, it's me. I'm over here," I replied.

Soon we were together and it was time for roll call. "By the number," I said, starting the count to ensure everyone was present.

"Okay, we're all here," Ted said. "Now remember we've got to be quiet, especially as we move by security location."

"Come on. Let's get started. We've gone through this before," Gary said as we were all anxious to move out.

"Just be careful," I said. "Let's make sure that we all stay together."

Everything was going as planned. We were moving forward across the rugged terrain when the talking started. "Take it a little slower up there," Bill called from the back. "We're having trouble keeping up."

"It's so dark and all the roughness, we'd better slow it down a little," Shane said.

"Wait up!" I heard someone call. I stopped and listened.

"Number one, wait up. We've got problems," Bill's voice sounded.

We waited until Bill and some of the others got to us. "What's the trouble?" I asked, hoping that we weren't separated.

"I think we've lost part of our group," Bill said.

"Are you sure?"

"I'm not sure. We'll have to take a count to find out."

"We should have started earlier," Ted remarked as we stood waiting and listening, isolated from each other by the thick walls of darkness.

"What're we going to do?" Shane asked.

"There's no use waiting any longer. We might as well take roll call," Ted said.

"Again by the number, fellows," I replied as I started the count.

"Number twelve, that's William. We've lost him," Bill said.

"We didn't plan for this. What do we do now?" Henry asked.

"You want me to try and locate him?" Gary asked.

"No. You all stay here. I'll try to find him."

"But without a light, you'll never get back to us," Shane said.

"That'll be no problem. Here take the end of the twine," I said as I handed it to Shane.

"What's this for?" Shane asked.

"It's just to make sure I get back," I replied, holding the ball of twine in my hand.

"Don't lose any time. We haven't got many hours left," Robert said.

"I'll be back soon as I can." I started moving back in the direction from where we came, listening and hoping that I would hear William's voice. For more than twenty minutes I moved back down the rugged terrain. Twice I stopped and called. Still there was no sound from William, only the noises from the sea. I began to get a little nervous, knowing that William might have lost his bearing and went in the direction of the cliffs. I kept moving and the twine was winding down. Finally I stopped again and stretched upward straining as I called William's number loudly. I waited. A second was like an hour.

"Over here, I'm over here," William's voice sounded anxiously. Then the two of us talked as we moved toward each other. Finally we were together. "Boy! Am I glad to see you," William said.

It was dark and we couldn't see each other but that was no concern. We had the comfort of being together.

"You fellows got away from me," William said.

"We didn't realize you were lost. What happened?"

"I stopped to take a leak and then I tripped and fell and sprained my ankle. The first thing I realized you all were gone and I couldn't hear anyone."

"Are you sure it's only a sprain?"

"Yeah. It hurts a little but I can make it. I'm still able to walk on it."

"Here," I said as I handed William the end of the twine.

"We didn't know we would use the twine for this, did we?" William remarked happily, as we walked along and slowly wound the twine up.

"How's the ankle?" I asked.

"It hurts some, but I'll be okay."

We kept moving along slowly and then as we got closer, I could hear a little noise from the fellows.

"You made it," Gary said, his voice ringing through the darkness.

"What did you expect. I've been here long enough to know this mountain pretty well."

Quickly we started moving. I knew as we walked along that once we got the lumber, Sergeant Dooley wouldn't ask for it back. He knew the major was supporting us.

"Here we are, all the lumber we need," Ted said as we felt the lumber with our hands.

Having less time than expected and experiencing the roughness of the terrain, we decided to change plans. Rather than go around the mountain, we would take the risk and go straight across, near the N.C.O. Club.

"It's going to be dangerous going straight across," Shane remarked.

"But we don't have any other choice, Shane. There's not enough time left."

"Let me say something," Ted remarked, speaking quietly as he got everybody's attention. "This is Saturday night and with the plans changed we're going straight across, very close to the N.C.O. Club. That means we'll have to be very quiet and if you hear anyone, be sure to stop dead still in your tracks."

"We've got you," Gary replied, displaying his excitement.

With it being Saturday night and the lights still on at the N.C.O. Club, everyone understood the importance of what Ted said.

"It's been a coon's age since I felt like this." Henry said with a little laugh.

"And just to think we're doing this to build a chapel," I heard Russell say.

"It's ready fellows. There's six stacks tied off and this is the first of three trips. You know the plans. Ted and I will carry the first stack."

"We understand," Robert said as we began to move out.

With a feeling of excitement and hope for the future of the chapel, the first trip went off perfect. It was only when we started the second trip that several feet in front of us I heard a noise. Immediately I gave a little sound bringing everyone to a dead stop. We stood motionless, holding the lumber, hardly breathing as two sergeants came walking by just a few feet from us. For an eternity, it seemed, we stood for another few minutes, all tense, hoping that no one else would come along. Finally, we relaxed and started on our way. Just before dawn our mission was completed. We were totally exhausted and the excitement was gone. Everyone understood that taking the lumber for the chapel was wrong. But, with the major supporting us and knowing that someday we would return the lumber, we believed we were justified in what we did.

Chapter 9

It was Sunday morning and the long ordeal of getting the lumber was finally over. We were nervous, tired, and numb. Still, we met as usual for our regular Sunday morning Bible study. In the beginning of the study, prayer was given by Ted asking God for leadership and wisdom in the building of the chapel. Later when the study was completed, we all sang *Amazing Grace* and then Shane, Gary, and I walked to the chapel site.

"What do you think?" Shane asked as we stood viewing the lumber.

"It's not bad," I replied as I reached down, examining a few of the boards.

"But we haven't got enough boards to build the foundation form," Gary said.

"That'll be no problem, Gary. We'll set up and pour part of the foundation and then tear down and reset for the rest of it," Shane replied.

"That's what you hope," Gary remarked as he looked toward the N.C.O. Club.

"What do you mean hope? We've got enough money

to buy the cement and sand to get us started," Shane replied, almost irritated by Gary's pessimistic comment.

"That may be true, Shane, but how do you know we can keep the lumber?"

"Like we've said a hundred times, Gary, the major's behind us. That's why."

"Yeah, but suppose Sergeant Dooley asks us to return it, then what?"

Realizing that Shane was becoming more irritated by Gary's persistence, probably because of no sleep, I interrupted. "If Sergeant Dooley asks any questions, just send him to me. I'll take care of it."

"But it's obvious. If he doesn't already know, he'll know by tomorrow that we took the lumber."

"I know that, Gary, but if we never admit it outright, he'll be forced to go to the major and he won't do that."

"But it's like Ted said, we're in the army and with him a sergeant you know what that can mean."

"But that doesn't make any difference, Gary, not as long as we can go on with the chapel," I replied.

"Gary! We've been through this a thousand times," Shane said.

"But Jim will take the rap for all of us, Shane, and that won't be fair."

"If that's what it takes, that's okay. At least the chapel will be going up," I replied.

"But that wouldn't be right. We all took the lumber."

"I understand what you are saying, Gary, but we all made the decision for what we thought was best. Now we can go ahead with building the chapel. Besides Sergeant Dooley may never say anything."

"Shane's right, Gary. Don't worry about it." As we stood around a little longer, it was obvious that Gary was watching for Sergeant Dooley, thinking that he might come over. Finally we left the chapel site.

. . . .

"Is that you, Jim?" Simms asked as I opened the door and walked over to my bunk.

"Yeah, it's me."

"What time is it?" Simms asked, groaning at the thought of getting up.

"It's eleven-thirty."

"Eleven-thirty!" Simms snapped, jerking the blanket down and sitting up.

"There's no problem, Simms. Today is Sunday."

"You're not kidding me, are you?" Simms asked, knowing that he usually depended on me to get him up.

"No, I'm not kidding you. All that drinking all the time, it's going to get you if you keep on."

"Maybe I'll die and my problems will be over," Simms said as he got out of bed and sat on the side of his bunk.

"But I know you love your family and they need you different from the way you're going," I said as I watched him reach under his bunk and start the day off with another bottle.

Simms was listening to what I said and the redness shone on his face as he lowered the bottle from his lips. Then he turned and gazed at the canvas. Appearing to realize he had a problem, he placed the partially empty bottle back under his bunk and then he stood up and walked over and picked up Duke's Bible. There he stood with the answer to his problems, but he never opened the Bible. He put it down and walked toward the door.

"You know, Jim, about my family, maybe you're right," he said and then he walked on out the door.

Simms was gone. It was just Gimp and me sitting alone, the two of us sharing the emptiness of the hut. "Gimpy, old boy, we're making progress," I said as I slid off the bunk and got down next to him. "We've got the lumber just like we planned and now we're going to build the chapel just like we've planned it. And you know something else, old fellow," I said, stoking his fur, "you're getting better. You may never be the same but you're going to be back out on the mountain again. Out there roaming it, living life the way it's suppose to be, down on the mountainside with the boys and Tom, having a good time. That's the way it's supposed to be, fellow. Not like this, not in here all cooped up under this canvas. But I know sometimes for all us it gets to be too much, especially for fellows like Simms. So you see, boy, there's all the reason in the world for you to get better. There are things that you and the children can give us that sometimes we can't give one another. Listen, Gimpy, we've got company," I said when I heard Ted's voice as he knocked on the door.

"Young'un, are you in?" Ted asked.

"Yeah. Come on in."

Just as the door opened, I knew from Ted's expression that something was wrong.

"What's up?" I asked.

"Come on! Come on with me and I'll show you."

"But what's wrong, Ted?"

"Just come with me and I'll show you."

I wondered if something drastic happened at the club and Ted wouldn't tell me. Soon I realized it had something to do with the chapel. "This way," Ted said, changing our direction slightly.

"It's Sergeant Dooley, isn't it?" I asked.

"Yeah. Look, you can see for yourself," Ted remarked as we were standing in an obscured position from the chapel site.

"That's him! That's Sergeant Dooley all right. He's already over there."

"He didn't lose much time, did he?"

"Not at all, but I'm not surprised, are you?"

"Just that this being Sunday, I thought it might be another day or two. You're nervous, aren't you?"

"Not really nervous, Ted, but maybe a little concerned. Even though the major is supporting us, some way we'll need the cooperation of everyone, even Sergeant Dooley if we can get it."

"But you're going to take the rap, Young'un. You know that."

"Maybe and maybe not. We'll have to wait and see."

"But you know Sergeant Dooley."

"It doesn't really matter, Ted. If everybody will do as we've said, we can go on building the chapel."

"But . . . "

"But that's the only way, Ted. The only way unless we admit taking the lumber and we're not going to do that. That'd be the end of the chapel.

"I know what you're saying and I realize it's got to be that way but I still . . ."

"No but about it, Ted. It's like you told Shane, everything is going just as planned and let's keep it that way. Anyway, like I said, this may be the end of it. Sergeant Dooley may never say anything." Ted and I stood watching Sergeant Dooley, wondering what was going through his mind.

"Look! He's leaving. He's going toward post engineers."

"I just hope we've done the right thing, Young'un."

"There's no problem, Ted. Sergeant Dooley will do what he has to and we'll go on with the chapel.

"What about the sand? Have you checked with Sergeant Barrett to see if we can get the trucks?"

"Not yet. I was waiting until we needed them."

"But you know we may have more problems, don't you?"

"You mean because of Sergeant Dooley. You think he'll say something to Sergeant Barrett?"

"It could be, and then too, Sergeant Barrett might be like Sergeant Dooley and you know what that'd mean."

"Yeah. I hadn't thought about that, but you're right."

"This is just the beginning, Young'un. Even if we get the trucks, there'll be all kind of problems before it's finished."

"We knew that, Ted. And we knew that we can't antici-
pate all the problems, but we've buckled to it, first with blis-
tered hands and now the lumber. So we've got to keep going."

With a feeling of numbness I left Ted and walked down
on the mountain side. There I took time to view the beauty
of the sea, to watch the rippling of the waves and the little
boats going to and fro as they were being skillfully guided
to move with the forces of nature. Then I looked upward
into the sky. There I saw the beauty of God's creation as the
clouds drifted along the way. Off to my right I could see
Tom and then down below him I could see the old man
who seemed to have his place on the mountainside. Tom
had his back turned to me as I walked up.

"Boo!" I said, slipping up behind him.

"Jim! I wasn't expecting you," Tom said as he lowered
the harmonica. "The old man over there, you see him?" Tom
asked. "He's a retired seaman. Often times he's looking out
across the sea watching the ships and recalling a life of good
times."

Tom and I just started walking toward him. It seemed
a natural thing to do. As we got closer to the old man, I
could see a lifetime of work in his sunken eyes embedded
within the wrinkles and his slumped shoulders. He stood,
thin, with a balding head, his clothes wrinkled and worn.
Like an old building with no one to care for it, he stood
alone.

"*Merhaba*," the old man said, smiling as he was telling
us hello.

"*Merhaba*," Tom responded and then Tom turned and
pointed toward me. "Jim," he said letting him know that
my name was Jim.

"Jim," the old man replied.

"*Evet*," I replied, letting him know he pronounced my
name correctly.

"Hasan," the old man said, pointing to himself.

"Mehmet?" Tom asked, speaking to Hasan.

"Mehmet, *yok*," Hasan replied, letting Tom know that Mehmet was not around.

I looked at Hasan and his aging smile and then I looked at the youthful Tom, the three of us sharing a lasting moment together.

"*Orada*," Hasan called, breaking the silence as he pointed to a ship at sea.

Then as Tom pulled the harmonica from his pocket and started blowing I looked upward into the sky and saw the moon. So many miles apart and yet so close, I thought, as I felt the presence of home. Then as evening began to approach, Tom and I bade Hasan farewell and we turned and started up the mountain. Along the way we talked briefly about the lumber and what our expectations were for the future. Then with a good night's sleep and most of the day's work completed, I took time to go over to the motor pool to see Sergeant Barrett. Knowing the importance of the outcome, I was a little nervous as I passed by post engineers.

"Young'un, what brings you over?" Handley asked as I walked up in the motor pool.

"I need to see Sergeant Barrett. Is he around?"

"Yeah, he's standing over yonder. Would you like for me to call him?"

"No, there's no use in doing that. I'll just wait," I replied. I walked over and was examining one of the wrecked trucks, having thoughts that eventually the frame could be salvaged and used as structural steel in an upper portion of the steeple. When I turned around, Sergeant Barrett was walking toward me. Momentarily I became nervous, wondering if he already knew about the lumber. Then, somewhat surprisingly, he smiled and spoke in a gentle voice.

"Handley said you wanted to see me."

"Yes, Sir. I don't know whether anyone has told you or not but several of us are trying to build a chapel."

"Yeah, I've heard a little talk about it. So you're the ones that are building the chapel?"

"Yes, Sir. We're trying to but we're having a lot of difficulty. We've located some sand and gravel and we were wondering if we could use some of the trucks."

"Some of our trucks?"

"Yes, Sir. We need them for hauling the sand and gravel, if we can use them."

"I don't know, Boyte. We're pretty busy using them. I'm sure that you understand that."

"Yes, Sir. But what about in the evening hours and nights? Would there be any possibility of our using them then?"

Sergeant Barrett seemed a little puzzled, like he didn't know how to respond. "You fellows really want to build the chapel, don't you?"

"Yes, Sir. We believe there's a need for it. We first got the approval from the major but we don't have much money. We were hoping, if you could let us use the trucks, we could haul in enough sand and gravel to get the foundation started and then maybe the funding in contributions would increase."

"But evening hours and nights, that may be difficult on you," Sergeant Barrett replied.

"But that'll be okay, Sir. If you can let us use them," I said, and then I watched his expression and waited for him to speak. Unlike Sergeant Dooley he seemed concerned for us.

"You're right, Boyte. This mountain needs a chapel," he said and then paused. Finally he spoke again, "There shouldn't be any problem in the evenings and at night."

"You mean it will be okay?"

"Yeah, I don't see any problem. I'll tell the dispatcher so that he'll understand."

"Thanks! Thanks a lot, Sergeant."

"You don't need to thank me. It's all for a good purpose."

"But thanks anyway."

"Sure thing and if you run into any problems just let me know."

"Okay, and we sure do appreciate it. Thanks again."

I was all excited with the news and anxious to share it with the rest of the fellows as I started back to the chapel site. I was hurrying along when I came up over the knoll and suddenly stopped. I was sure that it was Sergeant Dooley. He was standing with the other fellows. At first I wanted to turn and go in the opposite direction but then a source of strength came and I slowly walked on.

"Jim, Sergeant Dooley wants to see you," Shane said as I walked up.

"Good evening, Sergeant," I spoke, trying not to show my nervousness.

Sergeant Dooley was looking at the lumber. He turned around, all two hundred pounds in his short stocky build. At first with a calmness, his shoulders were slumped as he looked at me. Then his eyes began to penetrate with a fierceness and his shoulders stiffened upward as a burning redness began to show on his face. Like a lion he stood paused, ready to attack, while I stood strengthened for the blow.

I waited. His eyes didn't flinch. He stood firm. Finally in a subdued voice, his throat tightened and he spoke.

"Boyte," the sound came.

"Yes, Sir."

"There's just one thing."

"What's that, Sergeant?"

"You know what I'm talking about," he said as he turned back facing the lumber.

"You seem upset. When I first saw you, I was hoping you came over here to tell us we could borrow some lumber. We managed to get this but we need more."

"What are you saying! Are you trying to tell me this lumber didn't come from post engineers?"

"I don't know whether the fellows told you or not . . ."

"You trying to tell me you didn't take this lumber? You don't think I'm stupid, do you?"

"No, Sir. I know you are in charge of post engineers."

"That's right and the two of us know the truth. You just remember that."

Sergeant Dooley didn't say anything else. He took one last fiery look at me and then turned and walked away.

"He's gone," Bill said with a sigh of relief.

"Yeah, he's gone all right but it's not the end of it," Shane replied.

"Probably not. But we're going on up with the chapel. Just remember, don't ever admit we took the lumber."

"Something wrong?" Ted asked, walking up.

"Yeah. Sergeant Dooley was just over here," Gary replied.

"Sergeant Dooley! What'd he say?"

"He wanted to know about the lumber."

"So what did you tell him?"

"Nothing much. It's just the way he phrased his comments."

"He knows we took the lumber," Shane replied. "Just as he was leaving he said, 'You don't think I'm stupid, do you?' and he went on to tell Jim that he knew we took the lumber."

Watching Ted's expression, I knew that he was concerned. "It's okay, Ted. We did what we had to."

"I know, but it's just that I'm concerned about you, and then you know what we said about Sergeant Barrett."

"Sergeant Barrett! I've got some good news. I just came from the motor pool not long ago."

"Good news! It's about time we had some good news," Gary said.

"What did Sergeant Barrett have to say?" Ted asked.

"He said as long as we used the trucks in off duty hours there would be no problem."

. . . .

With Sergeant Dooley gone, we spent the next hour starting the foundation form. Then as night was approaching we were walking in when Ted stopped and looked back. "What do you think, Young'un?" he asked.

"It looks good, Ted. It looks like we've finally started," I replied.

"But such a long way to go," Shane replied.

"You're right, Shane, but we're going to see some real progress now," Gary remarked as we turned and started in.

"You fellows still at it?" Duke asked as I walked in.

"Yeah, we're still at it. We've finally started the foundation form," I replied as I walked over to Gimp. "How goes it, old Gimpy?" I said, gently rubbing his fur, watching him wag his tail.

"Looks like he's getting better," Duke remarked.

"Yeah. You're going to make it, aren't you, Gimpy? It won't be long and we'll take that splint off."

"It's not long for me either," Duke said with a smile as I looked over toward him.

"How many more days, Duke?"

"Just two more days and I'll be on my way home. It's kinda hard to believe that a whole year has come and gone."

"We're going to miss you, Duke. You know that."

"It almost seems like a dream," Duke said with his eyes focused on the replica of the chapel.

I watched Duke as he continued to look at the replica. Finally he spoke. "This place needs the chapel. Do you think you guys will ever get it built?"

"Not during the time we have left but we're hoping that if we can get the foundation in that those who come after us will complete it."

"The money is still the big problem, isn't it?"

"Yeah. If it's never finished, that will probably be the reason," I replied. Duke didn't say anything else. He just reached over and picked up one of his letters and lay across his bunk and started reading.

Soon the two days were gone. Duke and I stood enjoying the last few minutes together. "You made it, Duke a whole year of it and now you're leaving."

"But I'll always remember you," Duke replied as he reached out to shake my hand. Then he walked over to Gimp. "Gimpy, old boy, you take care," he said, reaching down, stroking his fur. Then like he didn't want to leave, he stood staring at the replica of the chapel. Finally he pulled out a twenty-dollar bill and dropped it in.

"You take care, Young'un," he said as he shook my hand again and then went out the door.

"He's gone, Gimpy," I said, feeling the loneliness as I sat staring at the nakedness of his bunk. I fed Gimp and hurried out thinking that I might get one last glimpse of the truck as it moved down the mountain. But my quick movements weren't fast enough. I could only hear the faint roaring of the engine as its sounds faded into the distance. For several months a closeness between Duke and the rest of us had developed and now it was over.

Throughout the day a loneliness prevailed. Later in the evening, I walked toward the chapel site.

"Young'un," Ted called.

"What's up?" I answered as he moved toward me.

"The cornerstone. It's all ready," he said with his eyes beaming and his face glowing.

"That sounds good," I replied.

. . . .

Sergeant Barrett was good for his word. The next evening eight of us were like a bunch of kids, taking our first ride down the mountainside. I was driving and the windshield and canvas top were lowered. Our radiant voices sounded with the songs of joy as we moved along. On through the village of Sinop and over the ox cart road we traveled. Finally the truck was positioned and with the strength of men we muscled the stone upward and carefully loaded it onto the truck. About thirty-five minutes later we arrived back at the chapel site and positioned the truck for unloading.

"Easy," Ted cautioned as we carefully slid the stone off and positioned it in the corner. Ted stepped back several feet and looked.

"What do you think, Young'un?" he asked in admiration.

"It looks great, Ted. Like I said before, it couldn't have been done better."

"Now if we can just get the foundation completed," Gary remarked.

In the evenings ahead, using Taner as our interpreter, we used two trucks, working into the late hours of the night hauling sand. Finally, with time of essence, enough sand was hauled in and we turned our attention to getting gravel. Having picked up Taner and leaving little Mehmet standing alongside the road, we were on our way to get the first load of gravel. I was driving the lead truck with Taner and Ted sitting up front with me. Shane was driving the truck following us.

"Are you sure the boy knows where he's taking us?" Ted asked.

"I know where we going," Taner replied.

"Have you been there before?"

"No, but I know where we going."

"Are you sure Taner knows where we're going, Young'un?"

"I think so, Ted. From what I understood Hasan to say, I think Taner can get us there."

"I get there," Taner replied again.

"There's one thing about it, Young'un, whether the chapel's ever finished or not, it's giving us something to do," Ted said as we traveled on down the dirt road.

"That's what I told the major when I first went to him. But we've got it going now, Ted. Someday the chapel will stand high on the mountain." For several miles we continued to drive. As I listened to the noise on the back of the truck, I knew that in part Ted was right. Building the chapel was giving us something to do.

"Look at the sunset. It's pretty, isn't it?" Ted remarked.

"Yeah. It's pretty and then the clouds and the beauty of the valley with the Turks harvesting their grain."

"One thing about it, just a few miles out from the mountain and it certainly looks different," Ted said.

We traveled on watching the beauty of the sunset fading into twilight.

"Are you sure that the boy knows where he's taking us?" Ted asked.

"I know where we go. Keep going," Taner replied.

"It's getting toward dark, Jim. What do you think?"

"I think we're okay," I replied with some question in my mind about the forks in the road some distance back. "Taner, back there. Are you sure we took the right road?"

"Yeah. Keep going."

"How far?" I asked.

"Maybe five kilometers."

"How far's that?" Ted asked.

"I'm not sure. Maybe about three miles."

"Look at that dark cloud, and it's beginning to rain."

"What I was afraid of," Ted remarked as the drops of rain were hitting against the windshield. Soon the cloud moved on and the rain stopped.

"The boy said only three more miles. We should be there, shouldn't we?" Ted asked.

"A little more," Taner replied with his head next to the windshield.

"We're at least forty miles out, Young'un. What do you think?"

"I'm not sure, Ted. We'll go just a little further."

"I don't know. Maybe too far," Taner said.

"What I was afraid of. The boy's not sure where he's taking us."

"I do know," Taner replied.

"It's so dark, Ted. I expect it's giving him some trouble."

"Are you sure we need to turn around, Taner?" I asked as I began to slow down.

"Yeah, back there!" he said anxiously pointing back in the other direction.

"Don't tell me we're turning around here!" Ted said as I nosed the front of the truck next to the edge of the road where it dropped off almost one thousand feet straight down the mountain.

"Yeah. Just hold on," I said as I eased the front wheels to the edge of the road. Several times we eased forward and then backward, moving only a short distance at the time. Finally we were turned around. "You can loosen up, Ted. We made it."

"I know we joke a lot, Jim, but this is serious business," Ted said wrenching his hands as Shane's truck eased up next to us.

"It's mighty close quarters, isn't it?" Shane remarked as our trucks came to a stop.

"It's too close," Ted said still appearing to be nervous.

"But we made it, Ted."

"I haven't turned mine around yet," Shane said.

"Would you like for me to get it, Shane?"

"No. I didn't learn to drive a truck for nothing. Just watch me and see," Shane said in a joking voice as he pulled off. Then as we sat waiting, it was obvious that he turned around much faster than we did.

With both trucks turned around, I began to move slowly down the road, trying to make sure we didn't miss the turn-off. As we rounded a curve I could see what appeared to be a little side road.

"Down there!" Taner said, pointing excitedly.

"You sure?" I asked, bringing the truck to a stop.

"Yeah. That building over there. That's how I know."

"It's not much of a road, Young'un. I don't believe the boy knows where he's taking us," Ted said as the fellows got off the back of the truck and came around.

"Are you sure it's down that way, Taner?" Tom asked.

"Yeah, we go down that way," Taner said emphatically pointing down the road.

"I'd say that we try it," Tom said. "I think he's taking us in the right direction.

"That's hardly a road. What if we get in there and can't get out?" Gary remarked.

"Gary's got a point, Jim. What do you think?" Shane asked.

"With all we've gone through before, we certainly won't let the roughness of that little road stop us."

"You all load up. We're going to get the gravel," Ted said.

Shifting into four-wheel drive, we began to slowly move forward. Using the winches a couple of times, we slowly traveled over the treacherous road for a distance of approximately four miles. Finally the excitement broke through as the lights shone on the gravel along the seashore. To the happiness of Taner, his determination brought us through.

"Rough as it was coming in, we'll never make it out," Shane said.

"But we've got to get the gravel. We've got to have it for the foundation."

"With it so dark and beginning to rain again, what are we going to do?" Gary asked.

"We'll have to load one truck at a time, using the lights from the other one to see by."

"You want to get mine first?" Shane asked.

"Yeah, if you'll pull up and back in, I'll turn around and shine my lights."

A cold rain was falling and everyone was anxious to get the trucks loaded. First Shane pulled up and then with the wheels spinning, the truck slowly moved back to the gravel. Then I positioned my truck so that we could see without being blinded by the lights. Finally when both trucks were in place we started loading.

"In years to come, they'll never know what we went through to build the chapel," Gary said.

"But that's okay, Gary. That's not the reason we're building it," Shane replied.

"I can assure you of one thing," Ted said.

"What's that?"

"We don't have to worry about a Sergeant Dooley out here."

Ted was right, we didn't have to worry about Sergeant Dooley. We were at least forty miles from the mountain, way out in the far reaches of Turkey, a long way from home. Yet, in the presence of God, all seven of us were wet and cold as we worked for more than two hours. Finally in the storminess of the night, when the last shovel full was loaded, we quietly took our places on the trucks. Soon the engines were roaring and the moaning sounded as the heavily loaded trucks began to move forward. In the soaking rain we traveled for more than one thousand feet and then the movement began to slow as the engine roared and the wheels were spinning.

"That's it," Ted said when the truck came to a stop. Then for the first time I watched, seeing some frustration as he opened the door.

"Just a minute, Ted, maybe if I can get it to rocking."

"It's no use. It's just not going any further, not until we hook the winch."

"But everything's so small, Ted. With this load, there's nothing to hook to."

"But we've got to do something, Young'un," Ted replied as he crawled out of the truck.

"What I was expecting," Shane said as he walked up.

I didn't know what we could do. I was sitting in the truck with the engine running and Taner was sitting beside me watching the windshield wipers go back and forth. Ted crossed in front of the truck, wading deeply through the mud.

"Come on, Jim. We can't stay here forever," Bill called, his voice shivering in the cold, dark hours of the night.

"We'll try the winch. Pull the cable out and hook it to the sapling up there."

"Okay," Shane replied as he and Ted took hold of the cable and began to trudge through the mud. I sat in the truck, watching them struggle through the mud, waiting for their signal.

"All right, it's all ready," Ted called, waving his hand.

"Make sure the cable's against the ground."

"Take it away. It's all ready," Shane called back.

The lights were glittering in the falling rain while everyone anxiously watched the cable. Then just as the cable began to tighten the voices of hope rang out. Quickly the engine began to roar and the wheels began to spin. Then all hope was silenced when the sapling gave way.

"We didn't move," Taner said.

"You're right. We didn't move," I replied as I reached over and patted him on the knee. Then I leaned forward against the steering wheel.

"What do we do now?" Gary asked still hoping for an answer.

I knew we had to do something. It wouldn't be many hours before we had to be back on the mountain.

"We could try the winch on the other sapling," Shane commented.

"But that would be no good, Shane. It'd be like the first sapling," Gary remarked.

"The way this rain's coming down, we've got to do something," Butch said.

Listening to what was being said and realizing the rain was falling harder, I knew we had to do something. "Let's try shoveling out from under the wheels. Maybe that way I can get it to rocking."

"Whatever you say," Ted replied, picking up a shovel.

We were all wet and cold and the anxiousness of the earlier hours was gone. Still most everyone was working, trying hard to get the truck moving.

"You about ready to try it again, Young'un?" Ted called from the other side.

"Yeah, anytime the rest of you are."

"Just a minute," Gary called, still shoveling at the front wheel.

"Is that it?" I asked, seeing him as he stepped back.

"Yeah, go ahead. Let's see what it's going to do, Young'un."

I put it in reverse and stepped down on the accelerator.

"It's moving! Keep it going," Gary shouted.

"Don't get too excited, Gary, the Young'un went in the wrong direction."

I brought the truck to a stop and we were ready to try it again.

"If you make it through, Jim, we'll catch you moving," Butch called out.

The rain was pouring as the engine roared.

"That's it! Keep it going! Keep it going!" echoed the voices, forcing the truck onward. Everyone was anxiously watching, hoping the truck would keep moving. Then all at once the engine kept roaring and the truck came to a stop with the wheels spinning.

"It's no good," Taner said.

"You're right. It's no good," I replied as I sat staring, trying to think of something else we could do. Then I got out of the truck.

"Looks like we've got company," Shane said observing a couple of the Turkish men braving the weather.

"All this rain and being so wet and cold, maybe if we take the gravel and fill up the ruts, then Shane can drive his truck up and push us."

"But that means we're going to lose the gravel," Gary replied.

"That may be, Gary, but some way we've got to get back to the mountain," Ted said.

Frustrations were running high as we stood around, wading through the mud. There was talk by some that we get in the cabs of the trucks and sit until the rain stopped but I knew that wouldn't work. We were in the military with jobs to do, and we had to get back to the mountain.

"It's going to take the wrecker or maybe more to get us out," Butch said.

"What're we going to do?" Gary asked.

"Like Jim suggested, there's only one thing we can do," Shane said.

"You mean unload the gravel from Jim's truck and fill up the ruts?"

"Yeah. That way I can pull my truck up on the gravel and push against Jim's truck.

"At least that's what you hope," Gary said as he reached down and started shoveling.

At the cost of giving up one load of gravel we made our way back to the main road. Then as we traveled down the road, all wet and cold, Taner was asleep and there wasn't much being said between Ted and me. Finally as we rounded the mountain, I could see a few lights down in the village of Sinop.

"We better wake the boy, hadn't we,?" Ted asked as we were nearing the village.

"Yeah, we'll soon be there."

"Wake up. Wake up, Taner," Ted called, reaching over and shaking his leg.

I knew Taner was tired and sleepy as he raised his head up and looked out the window. "We're in Sinop, Taner. Show me how to get to your house."

"Just up the road, Hasan's waiting for me."

"Hasan his father?" Ted asked.

"No. Hasan not my father. My father dead," Taner replied giving both of us an empty feeling.

"Up there," Taner said, pointing to an old building that could be seen dimly through the rising fog.

"But where's Hasan?" I asked, bringing the truck to a stop.

"You wait. I go look."

I opened the door and Taner stepped to the ground. Then Ted and I listened as Taner called Hasan's name.

"He's nowhere around," Ted remarked.

"He doesn't seem to be," I replied as Taner called again.

"See you later," he said and then he turned and quickly disappeared into the darkness.

"He didn't give us a chance, did he?" Ted remarked.

"He's a brave little boy," I replied, seeing the lights from Shane's truck as he came into sight. I eased out on the clutch as the engine roared and we began to move up the mountain.

. . . .

It was 0345 hours when we arrived at the chapel site. I positioned my truck so we could have a light to see by. Then with only one truck to unload, Shane backed in and we started shoveling. When we were about halfway unloaded the rain had stopped and I could see a few stars and the moon shining through the breaking clouds. Finally at 0500 hours the trucks were parked and I was walking toward my hut. Along the way I stopped and looked up at the stars and the moon shining in the heavens above. I turned my head and the best I knew how I looked in the direction of home and then back up at the shining moon.

You remember what you told me, Dad, just as I was leaving. Well, there it is, shining brightly where God put it for you and me. So often I don't write home but if you only knew how often I look up into the heavens above and felt your presence with me, you would be pleased. I told you not long ago that I would share the chapel with you as we went along and I'm going to do that. Right now we're wet and we're cold and we're having a hard time getting the foundation in, but you and Mom always taught me that the good things in life aren't always easy, and then, Dad, I know how much you and Mom would like for me to be home, but as in a few hours the moon shall briefly fade out of sight, so shall we, in time to come, briefly fade away. But you and Mom helped to lead me to our home where we shall never fade away. So understand, Dad, as we're building this chapel, we're building it together and we're building it as our home for God and for mankind, that we shall never fade away from the gift of God's love that binds us together. Thanks, Pop, for all that you have given me, and now my Father in heaven, I thank You for the greatest gift of all, the gift of love. The love that binds us one to the other on this earth. The love in Your Son Christ that brings us home with You so that we shall never fade away into eternal death.

Chapter 10

———◆———

S oon our work would stop and we would have to wait for another payday to buy more cement. I was on the way to my hut, carrying some meat for Gimp, when I looked down on the mountainside, thinking I might see Tom. He would soon be leaving and I knew how much having a little time with the boys meant to him.

As I opened the door, I held the meat in front of me expecting to see Gimp's quick effort to stand up and try to come to me. Only a few days prior, he managed to stand up with the splint on and take a few steps. Suddenly when I looked down, I knew something was wrong. "Gimpy, boy," I called, anticipating some noise somewhere from him. With no sound, "Gimpy! Gimp! Gimp, boy!" I called louder. Thinking that he might be under one of the bunks I quickly I got down on my knees. "Gimp! Gimp, boy!" I called. Knowing he was nowhere around I quickly opened the door and stepped outside, again calling without any response. I walked around the huts, thinking that I might see some sign of him. He was nowhere around. I went back in the hut and looked for the splint. It was not there. Hurriedly I walked toward the chapel site, thinking that one of the fellows might have carried him over.

———◆———

"Something wrong, Young'un?" Ted asked, obviously sensing that something was bothering me.

"I don't think anything is really wrong. Some way Gimp got out of the hut."

"You mentioned that he was trying to walk a little. Do you think the door was left open and he might have got out?"

"I'm not sure, but I've got to find him. If he gets off and gets hung up with that splint on, it could really hurt him."

"We'll get this batch poured and then if you don't find him, let us know and we'll help you look for him."

Knowing that darkness would soon be on us, I anxiously turned and hurried off in the direction of the mountainside, down where Tom and the boys usually were. A few minutes later I sat down and watched as on down at a further distance I could see Tom, the boys, and Gimp. I just sat on watching. At first I had thought of concern for Gimp. But as I watched his movements and their joyful play I knew the moments of pleasure were well worth the little risk involved for Gimp. Then I walked down a little further and stopped again. I wanted to call out, to call Gimp's name. But just as I was about to speak, I saw the wobbly movements of Mehmet, his gentle touch on Gimp and then I watched Tom move over and sit down between the two of them. I didn't say anything. I didn't move. I just kept looking. Finally I looked at the redness of the sky and knowing that it would soon be dark, I turned and started up the mountain.

"You found him," Shane said.

"Yeah. He was over on the mountainside with the boys and Tom."

"With Tom? What about the splint?"

"It was gone. There was no sign of it anywhere."

"So Gimpy finally made it."

"Yeah. He's still a little wobbly, but he's back out there where he belongs."

"How do you like it, Young'un?" Ted asked as I was viewing the evening's work.

"It looks good, Ted, like we're finally getting somewhere."

"If we just had enough money."

"Yeah, I know, but some way we'll make it."

"Don't hurt yourself, Young'un," Ted remarked as I reached to pick up a shovel.

"You know me. I wouldn't do that."

"You're too late. This is it," Butch said pouring the last shovelful into the foundation.

"Til another payday," Shane said.

"But we'll make use of the time. We'll haul in more sand and gravel."

"We're not going to have any slack, are we, Young'un?"

"Not if we can keep at it. We need to make as much showing as possible."

"Maybe someday, Young'un, our hopes will be realized."

"Yeah, someday."

"See you fellows tomorrow," Shane said as he turned and walked off.

I went back to my hut and sat on the bunk. As I looked down at the floor where Gimp usually lay and I looked over at Duke's bunk, where it still remained empty, it all seemed so lonely. I kept waiting, thinking that Tom and Gimp would soon come back. Finally I lay across my bunk. Sometime later in the night I was awakened by a noise at the door. I listened for just a moment and realized it was Gimp. He was back. Quickly I got up and opened the door. "Gimpy, old boy," I said, reaching down to stroke his fur, "it's been a long time." Then feeling the closeness with him lying next to me, I turned over to go to sleep.

. . . .

The next morning I was awakened by a knock at the door. It was Dennis from supply and a new fellow coming in to take Duke's bunk. I got out of bed and slid my trousers on.

"My name is Jim Boyte," I said, reaching out to shake his hand.

"Wicker, Ralph Wicker is my name."

A few minutes later Ralph and I were on our way to the wash house when I noticed he had stopped. I didn't say anything as I watched him. He was turning, viewing the sea, looking off in the far yonder.

"So this is it. This is Sinop," he said.

"Yeah. This is it. Up on the mountain and down in the valley, a view as far as you can see."

"And this is where, many years ago, Caesar stood and made his famous statement, 'I came, I saw, I conquered.'"

"Yeah. That's what they say."

"How long you been here?" Ralph asked.

"Almost nine months," I replied, realizing I was becoming one of the old-timers.

Ralph turned and looked at me. His eyes looked bigger. "Nine months. That's a long time," he said and then he turned and looked off. "Is this place as bad as they say?" he asked.

"That all depends. It gets lonesome at times. They probably told you back in the states that we can't even talk to a girl over here."

"Yeah. That's what they told us. It doesn't matter anyway, I have a wife and a child back home."

I watched Ralph, his eyes continuing to view the surrounding. Soon the two of us walked on to the wash house and from there to chow.

. . . .

Several days passed and even though we had no money, we were back out on a Saturday afternoon with the trucks.

"What's wrong, Young'un?" Ted asked, as again we were trying to make our way in with more gravel.

"Plenty's wrong, Ted."

"You mean we've got real problems this time?"

"Yeah, real problems. With all the bouncing of the clutch, trying to get through the mud holes we've burned the clutch out."

"So what do we do?"

"There ain't but one thing we can do. You all go ahead and take the other truck in. See Sergeant Barrett when you get there and have him send the wrecker out."

"But this being Saturday, you know Sergeant Barrett, the way he drinks."

"If he's drunk, see Handley. We'll have to get the wrecker."

"But what about you, Young'un? What are you going to do?"

"I'm going to stay here. I'll need to stay with the truck."

"The couple of Turks we've been seeing at different times, aren't you afraid to stay by yourself?"

"No, I don't think there's any reason to be afraid."

"If you'd like, one of us could stay with you," Ralph said.

"There's no use in that. We have enough problems as it is. At least the rest of you can go on to work."

"Whatever you say," Butch replied.

Soon I stood watching them board the truck, knowing what it would mean if regular duty assignments were missed. A few minutes later I heard the roaring of the engine as I watched the truck slowly pull off. With everyone gone I felt the emptiness of my surroundings. I stood on for a few minutes with my boots sunk into the mud, listening to the truck, hoping that it would keep moving. Then the familiar sound started as the engine was roaring and the wheels were spinning. Soon it came to a stop and I began to trudge through the mud, trying to get to them. Finally I could see the truck. Still they hadn't noticed me as I walked closer.

"It's no use. I just don't think we can get it out," I heard Shane say.

"We'll make it some way," I said as I walked up behind them.

"Jim! We weren't expecting you," Shane said, as he turned quickly to face me. "You can see that we're bogged way down," he said as we walked around the truck.

"You're right. Even with the gravel we previously put in, it still went down," I said as I picked up the shovel and started shoveling.

"We're ready. Let's try it," Bill called a few minutes later.

I watched Shane as he got in the truck. First he tried to go forward and then backward. "It's just not going," Shane said, showing his frustration as he got out of the truck.

"We might as well start walking," Bill said.

"It's forty to forty-five miles. That's a long way across the mountain," Gary replied. "And just to think, it's already 1500 hours. We'd be walking a big part of the night and without any kind of protection, anything could happen to us."

"But anything could happen to us here," Ralph said as Shane was walking to the other side of the truck.

"Taner's calling you, Young'un," Gary said as I heard him call my name.

"Look! There's some other Turks with him," Bill said.

Bill was right. When I looked over, I saw Taner with four Turkish men, their oxen, and ox carts. I wondered what he wanted with me. "*Merhaba*," I said walking up with a smile.

"*Merhaba*," they responded in a pleasant voice.

"Em," Taner said as he always did in trying to speak my name.

I knew from his expression, there was something he wanted to tell me.

"What is it?" I asked.

"My friends, they want to help."

"But you know we can't push the truck out," I said, thinking that some way or other they thought we could manually push the truck out.

"No! Not push. Not that way. They want to use oxen."

"Oxen! You mean use the oxen," I replied as I looked over at the huge oxen.

"Oxen. You know, pull truck," Taner responded with a voice of strength.

"You might have something. That might work," I said as I walked over to where the Turkish men were. It was obvious as Taner started talking with them that they wanted to help and they were equally proud of their huge oxen.

"What're they up to?" Ted asked as he walked up, again showing his frustration when he spoke.

"Maybe something good. They'd like to hitch their oxen to the truck and try to pull us out."

"But look at them. They're only double team yoked and that means they can only hitch one team at a time and even then if we unload all the gravel they couldn't pull it out."

"I don't know, Ted. You've heard the old expression, strong as an ox, and those are huge oxen. They're not anything small. Besides, we don't have anything to lose."

"They can pull it," Gary said, interrupting the conversation between Ted and me.

"They pull?" Taner asked.

"Yeah. After we unload the gravel we'll let them try it," I replied. Then I listened, watching their smiles as Taner talked with them, knowing they were pleased to have an opportunity to help.

"What are they doing?" Shane asked as the Turkish men were engaged in serious discussion.

"They're trying to decide which team of oxen to use."

As they continued their discussion we started unloading. Two hours earlier it was the joy of voices singing and now it was the voices of frustration. Finally the gravel was unloaded and the oxen were hitched. I was walking toward the oxen when I heard Bill's voice.

"Wonder what they'd say if they knew all this were for a Christian chapel," Bill said.

"They know. I told them," Taner replied with an expression of satisfaction, knowing he was being involved in what was happening.

I looked everything over. The yoke was strong and the oxen were huge. The old Turk had his jabbing stick in a fixed position and Shane had the accelerator moving downward as the engine was revving up. "Tell him now, Taner. We're ready." Then just as Taner spoke, all forces were directed forward. At first it appeared the truck was going to move but it was just too much. The truck was bogged down too far.

"What I told you, Jim. I didn't think they could pull it out," Ted said.

"Maybe not," I replied as I watched the old Turk hollering and jabbing the oxen, forcing them to strain every muscle in their body. I continued to watch for a few more minutes, becoming somewhat concerned that the oxen might get hurt.

"Like I said, Young'un. It's just not going to work," Ted remarked.

"Taner, it's not going to work. Tell them to stop before the oxen get hurt."

"Maybe a little more," Taner said as the oxen continued to dig in.

"No. Now. Tell them to stop." Then I watched and listened as Taner brought everything to a halt.

"We might as well start walking," Ted said, all frustrated from the long days work and now the loss of time by trying to use the oxen.

I knew as I looked around and listened that there was good reason for the frustrated comments. Many of the fellows, including Ted, spent the night before listening in on the Soviet Union and now they were in their second day with little sleep. What was supposed to have been a day of joy away from the mountain now appeared to be a forty-mile hike back.

I looked over and saw the Turkish men again engaged in serious discussion. Shortly they broke from their discussion and started talking with Taner.

"Em," Taner called as they began to walk toward me.

"What is it?" I asked in a fretful voice.

"They get truck out. Use six oxen."

"Six oxen! Are you sure?"

"Yeah. They go home. Then come back."

"All of you heard that. What do you think?"

"If they can hitch six oxen, that ought to do it," Ted said, becoming a little more relaxed.

"What about the rest of you? What do you think?"

"It's too late in the evening to start walking. We might as well give it a try," Gary said.

"Taner, tell them okay. We will try the oxen again." Then again I watched their smiles of pleasure as Taner conveyed the message. Soon the oxen were hitched back to their ox carts.

"Em," Taner called as he started to walk with them.

"What is it?" I asked.

"We go eat. You heard cannon. We can eat now."

I understood what Taner was saying. It was the Ramadan fasting season for the Muslims and they had gone all day without food. Now the cannon had sounded letting them know they could eat.

"Come on, everybody hungry. They say you come."

"Are you sure, all eight of us?"

"Yeah. Everybody hungry. We all eat."

It was obvious from the quick reaction that all eight of us were hungry as we joined in the long muddy walk. This was a first. I knew of no other time that any American had been invited into a Moslem home.

We kept walking, even at times struggling to pick up

the weight of the mud as we moved forward. I couldn't understand what the Turks were saying but their pleasure was obvious as we slowly moved on.

"It's going to take all night if we don't soon get there," Ted said.

"At least we'll have something to eat," Shane replied.

"Taner, how much further?" I asked.

"We soon be there, over the next hill," Taner replied after asking the old man.

For more than two miles we had slowly traveled through the deep mud, following the Turkish men with their ox carts loaded with wood. Now as we started up the long hill I watched the oxen, almost straining as they pulled their loaded ox carts through the deep ruts of mud. Then I looked around and saw the tiredness of everyone. No one was speaking, only straining like the oxen to move forward. Finally, when we crested the top of the hill and started downward, one of the old Turkish men turned to me and pointed to an old, small two-story frame building.

"We stop here," Taner said as the team of oxen turned to the left, next to a brush fence with a poled gate. As we passed through the gate I stopped to examine the brush fence made of interwoven branches, stacked to about five feet.

"The other Turks, where're they going?" Gary asked.

"They go on, come back later," Taner replied.

"Are you sure we want to eat here?" William asked, looking at the conditions of the house and surroundings as we walked up.

"We eat here. You like food," Taner replied.

William's comment came as of no surprise. Shortly after arriving in Turkey, we all learned that for many of the farmers, the house in which they lived also served as the barn to house their animals. No exception was the house that we were now going to eat in. Wading through all the mud and smelling the sour odor as we approached made conditions appear even worse.

"Are you sure we want to eat here?" William asked again.

"I don't know about you, William, but I'm hungry," Gary replied.

I understood William's concern. First it was the sour odor and then the odor from the animal stalls.

Much to William's surprise, the evening became an enjoyable one. With the oxen placed in their stalls and fed, we followed the instructions of the old Turkish man. First we sat on the side of an old porch and removed our boots and then we went to a wash basin where we washed our hands. From there, as we walked back along the porch and started up the stairs it was evident that additional food was being prepared. A few boards squeaked along the way and I noticed William reach down to examine one of the boards before stepping on it. Soon we were in a small room, seated on homemade benches positioned around the walls. In the dimness as I looked at the hand-planed lumber, it reminded me of the one room where our family of six once lived. A short time later, two small boys brought in lanterns and lit them and then later the same two boys came back and placed a round swivel table about ten inches high in the middle of the room. As Shane looked at me without saying anything, I knew he was wondering what next.

Finally, almost one and a half hours after we arrived, the food was brought in and we followed the actions of the old Turkish man as we got up and went over and folded our legs, taking our positions next to the table. I looked over at Shane and then in silence I bowed my head and gave thanks. The old man smiled and started turning the table as the food was taken off. While everything was rough and crude, the cleanliness, the variety, and the taste of the food was outstanding. Occasionally, as I looked over at William, it was obvious he was enjoying the meal. Finally the eating was over and we stood up and started toward the door, thinking we were ready to leave.

"Look at that!" Shane said excitedly, pointing out the window. Quickly I moved over and looked out the window. Down below us I could see the movement of many lantern lights and then the door opened and the room filled with Turkish men. The eight of us sat back down on the benches and listened very quietly to their serious discussions. I finally turned and asked Taner what they were talking about. He said they were talking about their oxen and how they were going to pull the truck. To our dismay, we sat on for approximately another hour as they continued to talk. Then we began the long journey following the oxen and the Turks back to the truck. Finally when the six oxen were hitched up we were so tired that little reaction was shown when the truck started to move. At approximately 0300 hours we were back to the main road.

I wanted to go with them but I knew that I couldn't. In the darkness, with the moonlight shining, I stood listening to the truck move down the road. Then, with my limited knowledge of the Turkish language, I gave thanks to the Turks for all of their help and to the older gentleman for the evening meal. Finally I turned and started the long walk back to the truck. I was so tired, muddy and exhausted that I wanted to stop and sit down but with all the mud and it being so wet, I knew that I couldn't. At last, just in front of me I could see the truck. As I opened the door and started to get in, I was startled when I looked over at the other side and saw the passenger door swinging partially open. I knew the doors were closed when I left. Suddenly, at a distance of about two hundred feet, I saw the movement of at least one person. Quickly, I got in the truck and crouched down as I closed the doors. Then I took a small metal rod and held it out the window, hoping that with the moon shining it would give the appearance of a weapon. As the time passed it seemed clear that no one else was around. Yet I remained tense and tired, trying to stay alert as I held the rod. Finally it was daybreak and I began to relax as I watched the beauty of the horizon out on the sea. Into a moment of mediation I journeyed as I looked at the redness of the glowing rays, glistening like dancers to an audience unknown. Then later, like it was all a dream, l awakened to the sound of the wrecker coming in. It was Shane and Handley. I could see their smiles as the huge wrecker pulled up.

"I see you made it through the night," Shane said.

"And they tell me you tore the clutch out, Young'un," Handley remarked.

"Yeah. If I'm not badly mistaken, that's what happened."

"You sure it's not the transmission."

"I don't think so. I think it's the clutch," I replied as I watched Handley crank the truck up and try it. Then I watched him get out and look at the wheels to see how badly the truck was bogged down.

"Maybe you're right. This place is bad enough to tear up all the trucks."

"I just hope Sergeant Barrett doesn't get too upset. That's all we'd need."

"I don't think he will. He told us to work with you any way that we could. "

"Maybe if I'd taken a little more time and not bounced the clutch so much we wouldn't be in this mess."

"It won't be the last time, Young'un. Like I said, I don't think Sergeant Barrett will be too upset. Besides this is not the first time we've had it to happen. Now if I can just get this old five ton turned around," Handley said as he got in the wrecker.

"Just be careful. If we get that thing messed up we'll never be able to get another truck," Shane said.

As I looked at the dual wheels on the front of the big five ton, it was clear what Handley was talking about. All of the water we used on the mountain was hauled in from a distance more than forty miles away and often times, because of rugged conditions much like we were experiencing, the wrecker was used.

At first, as I watched the wrecker having some difficulty, I began to wonder if we were going to have to unload the gravel. Finally, Handley put the accelerator to the floorboard and the old wrecker sounded loudly as it moved us forward. I looked over at Shane. His tiredness was showing as he nodded off to sleep. Finally we were back on the mountain and Handley pulled the truck to the chapel site where we later unloaded the gravel.

It was late the next evening when I walked down on the mountainside with Tom and Gimp. I knew that in a few days Tom would be leaving and I wanted to have a little time with him. We were walking along when the boys came into sight. "There they are, like always," Tom said. Soon we were all together.

"Look at Mehmet, Jim. I just don't think he's going to make it," Tom said as I watched his stumbling movements.

"I don't know, Tom. Maybe he will," I replied, watching Taner reach over and help him along.

"It's just that I've got a hunch," Tom replied.

Soon it was like earlier times. The boys and Gimp playing while Tom and I sat talking. I kept watching Mehmet's efforts, thinking about what Tom said. Then I watched the gentleness of Taner as he reached down to help Mehmet up. Never to give up seemed to be his way of life as he was quickly playing again. Later twilight was on us and the sun was setting as Tom and I watched the boys and Gimp going down the mountain. Life has so much to offer, I thought as I watched Gimp turn and head back toward us.

Tom kept his eyes on the boys just as long as he could see them. Then reaching down to rub Gimp, he turned and spoke. "You know, Jim, the boys and Gimp, I almost wish I could stay on longer."

"Not many days to go, have you, Tom?"

"Only thirteen more and I'll be leaving."

"That's not very long."

"I know, and all the things I planned to do, like a lot of reading, I never got any of it done."

"But the boys and Gimp and then too, the sea and the mountains, I've always noticed you, Tom, you've never been lacking for something to do. You've always found something meaningful."

Tom started blowing the harmonica and Gimp started howling almost as if he sensed that soon Tom would be leaving. "Someday it'll be finished," Tom said as we walked up to the foundation.

"I'd like to think so, Tom, but all those obstacles we talked about, they're still all here."

"But God's with us. That makes the difference."

"You're right about that, Tom. But even with Him, it sometimes seems difficult."

"I know," Tom said, "but God didn't give us life so that everything would be easy."

"You know something about that, don't you, Tom?" I asked, thinking that he might say something. Finally he spoke.

"I guess life is different for all of us. For some there is a home to go to and then for some of us we just make home wherever we are. I know you've always seen me go out to mail call and wondered."

"You don't need to tell me, Tom, if you'd rather not."

"But I want to. You see when I was ten years old the only family I had, at least the family that loved me, was killed in a car wreck. You've talked about your twin brother. I had a brother too," Tom said painfully, with tears beginning to flood his eyes. Soon he was having difficulty talking. I reached over and placed my hand on his shoulder. He seemed to be weakened as he nervously moved his hands. I knew that at last his scar-torn youth was opening up. Finally he stopped trying to talk and just looked out across the sea. Then he started blowing the harmonica.

I wanted to say something but I couldn't, I just reached down and started rubbing Gimp's fur as I felt the pain flowing through the music. A few minutes later Ralph walked up.

"What're you guys up to?" he asked.

"The same old thing. We're killing time, waiting for another payday," Tom replied.

"What brings you over?" I asked.

"Sergeant Rollins came by the hut."

"Sergeant Rollins! What did he want?"

"I'm not sure. He asked where you were."

"Did he have anything else to say?"

"He just looked at your area. Said something about it being messy and then left."

"I wonder what he's up to," Tom remarked.

"And it was just my area?"

"Yeah. It was just your area. That's what I couldn't understand."

"Maybe it has something to do with Sergeant Dooley," Tom said.

"It wouldn't surprise me."

. . . .

It was several days later. Drizzling rain was falling. Tom and I were standing at the mail room waiting for the shutters to open.

"I guess this will be my last mail call," Tom remarked as we stood waiting like so many times before.

"One thing about it, Tom, one whole year has come and gone. Maybe you'll get that letter today," I said as the shutters opened.

"Boyte," the name sounded.

"That's me! Over here," I called as I stepped forward, reaching for the first letter to be handed out. Then I watched Tom, wondering what his thoughts really were as the shutters finally closed and the two of us walked off together.

"Listen to this, Tom. It's a letter from Mom and there's one from Dad, too."

I started reading. Mom and Dad were talking about Christmas. What it'd be like for us all to be home again, and then they asked about the chapel. When I finished reading I knew, as I looked at Tom, he was about to say something.

"Thanks for sharing your letters," he said.

"The letters are for both of us. You know that."

"The way your parents write and the way you are, I guess that's one of the reasons I kept coming out to mail call with you."

I knew Tom was hurting for love and I was glad to share the letters with him. "You need to go by and see my parents when you get back to the states. You'd like them and they'd like you too," I said as we walked over to the chapel site.

"I wish I could've done more," Tom said as he reached down and touched the cornerstone.

"But you'll always be part of it, Tom. You've helped us to overcome a lot of the problems. Maybe even the worst. I think once the foundation is completed the chapel will go on up."

"We have faced some problems, haven't we? But you know, they weren't all that bad. It gave us something to do. Maybe not what the major was expecting when we took the lumber but we got it anyway," Tom said with a smile. Then suddenly the smile disappeared. "I just hope Sergeant Rollins is not up to something."

"Don't worry about Sergeant Rollins, Tom. We're going on up with the chapel."

A few minutes later I stood looking at Tom and Gimp as they walked off. Tom wanted to know if I would go with him but I knew this was his last evening. The last few hours he would ever have with the boys and Gimp. Later he would be back at the club and I would join him there, I thought.

But later came and I kept waiting. Finally in the late-

---

ness of the night, I realized he wasn't coming. I thought of going by his hut but decided not to. With Gimp nowhere around, just maybe he was down on the mountainside, I thought as I walked on in that direction.

A short time later I paused as I listened to the flowing sound of the music. With the moon shining brightly, I walked a ways further where I could see Tom and Gimp sitting together. At first, with a thought that I would join them, I decided to stretch out on the ground for a few minutes and relax and enjoy the last of the music I would hear Tom play. As I lay listening to the music I wanted to capture the moment, to be able to keep it as part of my life. Thinking that soon I would walk on down, I was startled to realize I had drifted off to sleep. The music was gone. Only the stars were shining as I still listened, hoping for another sound of Tom. Through the darkness I felt my way back to the hut where I quietly undressed and crawled in my bunk. Then like so many times before, I awakened to the sound of Tom's voice.

"Jim, you awake?" Tom whispered trying not to wake the others.

"Yeah," I replied as I started to crawl out.

"Don't get up. There's no use in that. We're ready to leave. I just wanted to stop by and say good-bye and too, here's a bag of things I wanted to give you."

As I reached for the bag, Tom spoke again. "One other thing, Jim, if you don't mind, give little Mehmet this picture."

"We're going to miss you, Tom."

"You take care," Tom said as the door closed and I heard him speak for the last time. "Gimpy, old boy, you stay here. Jim will take care of you."

I lay awake, unable to go to sleep, knowing that Tom's presence would be no more.

Chapter 11

———■———

Through the passing of months, our closeness of friendships were established. While being confined to such a small area, we all knew the importance of our being on the mountain. On a continuous schedule, twenty-four hours a day, our mission was surveillance of the Soviet Union. Yet, the closeness of our friendships and the importance of our mission were not enough to overcome the loneliness. For some, getting drunk became routine. For others, spending time on the chapel, sometimes just talking about it, and having Bible study helped to fill the void.

Through the passing months I had watched the old-timers leave and the new fellows come in. Now day by day, like so many others, my time was becoming less. I stood with Gimp at the foundation, viewing the heavens above. I was confused, wanting to go home, yet like I'd told Tom, I wanted to see the chapel finished.

"Jim! Jim," Ralph called from a distance.

"What is it?" I answered, knowing something must be wrong.

"It's Sergeant Rollins. He wants to see you in the hut."

"Sergeant Rollins!"

———■———

"Yeah. He wants to see you."

"Any idea what he wants?" Shane asked.

"Your guess is as good as mine. I'll be back before long. Come on, Gimpy, let's go, fellow."

The door was open. I could see Sergeant Rollins as I walked in. "You wanted to see me, Sergeant " I asked, stepping inside.

"Is this your area?"

"Yes, Sir. It is."

"Your boots, do they always look like that?"

"No Sir, not all the time."

"But each time I've been by they're always muddy."

"Yes, Sir."

"But why, Boyte? You're in the army. You were taught different from that in basic training."

"Yes, Sir. I was."

"But look at them. Don't you see what I'm talking about?"

"Yes, Sir. And I do know that I'm in the army. I also know that excuses aren't acceptable."

"Are you trying to say that you have some kind of excuse?"

"No, Sir, not really. It's just that we're trying to build the chapel and sometimes we work late in the evenings on into the night."

"But what kind of excuse is that?"

"It's not an excuse, Sergeant. It's just that I have only two pair of boots and the pair you're talking about, they're still wet and muddy because I wore them last night."

"But like you said, that's no excuse."

"Yes, Sir, I realize that."

I didn't say anything else. I just watched as he looked back at my boots, and then he spoke.

"I expect we'd better do something about this. We can't let it continue. You do understand that, don't you?"

"Yes, Sir. I understand."

"So what do you think we should do?"

"Just whatever you say, Sergeant."

"Now you sound like you're in the army."

"Yes, Sir."

"A week from Saturday, you meet me over on the knoll beyond security location at 0800 hours. You understand?"

"Yes, Sir, I understand and I'll be there."

Sergeant Rollins was gone. I reached down and picked up my boot. Feeling its wetness, I placed it back. "Come on, Gimpy. It's time to go."

"What'd he say?" Ted asked.

"Nothing much. He just asked me about my area."

"That was all?"

"That was about it. He said something about my boots being muddy. He wants me to keep them shined."

"And we thought it had something to do with Sergeant Dooley," Shane remarked.

We were having enough problems as it was, so I didn't say anything else. I didn't want them to know. I just kept listening to the comments as we were working, knowing that it was just one of those days.

"No more than we're getting done, it's going to take a long time," Butch said.

"I'm just not sure it can be completed," Shane replied.

I understood what was being said. The frustrations were many and our time was becoming shorter. Still I wanted to see the chapel completed.

"What do you think, Young'un?" Ted asked.

"I still think once we get the foundation in and the walls started, it'll all be different then."

"But the weather is so bad and such a little money and then before long we'll be leaving. It just seems like everything is against us," Gary replied.

"But I still think if we stick with it, some day it'll be finished."

"But you know Ted's pulling out next week and it won't be long, most of us will be gone," Shane replied.

I didn't say anything else as I listened to what was being said. I knew what the feeling was like. I had experienced it many times. Later in the evening it was just Gimp and me as I sat on my bunk looking at the replica of the chapel. "Maybe they're right, Gimpy. Maybe it can't be done," I said, reaching down stroking his fur. "But we ain't going to quit, We're going to keep trying. There's too much need for the chapel for fellows like Simms and all the rest of us."

It was late Friday evening. Mail call was just over and I was on the way back to the hut. When I opened the door, I thought it was unusual for the time of day to see Simms sitting on his bunk.

I started to speak but then I noticed that he seemed different. He was staring at a picture. Moments later he raised his head. His sunken eyes were glassy, the redness showing when he spoke.

"Where you been?" he asked.

"Nowhere much. I just went down to the club for a few minutes and then decided to come back to the hut."

"Here. You want to see a picture of my family?" Simms asked, handing me the picture he was holding.

"You got a good looking family, Simms."

"But I'm no good. They don't want me anymore," Simms said, reaching to pick up his bottle.

"You've just been drinking a little much, Simms. Maybe when you get back home it'll be different."

"Not anymore. They don't want me anymore."

"But your children, Simms, I've heard you talk about them. I know from what you've said they love you and they need you."

"I wish that were true. But look at me. They're right. I'm no good. This evening, when I walked over to where you all are building the chapel I prayed. But it was just words. That was all. I couldn't feel anything, not like I used to."

"But you've got to keep on praying, Simms. And the Bible, we all need to read it more often."

"Would you read it now?"

"Yeah. I'd be glad to. Is there any particular scripture you'd like to hear?"

"It doesn't matter. You just pick out something."

"How about Psalms: 121. It's always been one of my favorites."

I will lift up mine eyes unto the hills, from whence cometh my help. My help cometh from the Lord, which made heaven and earth. He will not suffer thy foot to be moved: he that keepeth thee will not slumber. Behold, he that keepeth Israel shall neither slumber nor sleep. The Lord is thy keeper: the Lord is thy shade upon thy right hand. The sun shall not smite thee by day, nor the moon by night. The Lord shall preserve thee from all evil: he shall preserve thy soul. The Lord shall preserve thy going out and thy coming in from this time forth, and even for evermore.

I closed the Bible. Nothing was said for the next few minutes. Finally Simms raised his head. "About the chapel, how's it coming?"

"It's still slow but one of these days it'll be out there standing high on the mountain."

"I promised you I'd help and I still plan to."

"Any time. Just come on out."

Simms reached down and picked up his bottle. "You know, I thought I'd be going home to my wife and children, but the letter I got today, my wife is still asking for a divorce."

"But maybe it won't come to that, Simms."

"It already has. The last couple of letters, she's determined."

"But when you get back to the States, maybe it'll be different."

"Not any more. Just look at me. I'm no good."

Finally Simms was lying across his bunk. The bottle, lying empty, had taken care of his problems for a few hours.

I was up early the next morning, knowing that it was Saturday and Ted would be leaving later in the day.

"Young'un, over here, "Ted called as I walked into the mess hall.

"I've never seen you up so early on a Saturday morning, Ted."

"And you won't again."

"Give him a break, Young'un. You know this is his day," Bill said.

"But his truck's broken down. I was at the motor pool a few minutes ago. They said it would be tomorrow before it would be ready to leave."

"It's not in you, Young'un. You couldn't tell a lie if you wanted to," Ted said, joking me.

After chow Ted and I walked toward his hut. "It still doesn't seem real, Jim, but I guess I'm going home. You see my short-timer's stick. The last notch, I just put it in yesterday."

"It must be a good feeling, Ted."

"It seems good to be going home. You may have noticed that I didn't drink much at the club last night. When I left, I went over to where we're building the chapel and sat with Gimp for a long time. We may not be very far along with the chapel, but I want you to know what it has meant for me."

"Before you leave, come by the chapel site. There's something special we want you to do."

Ted didn't say anything. He just had an expression of wonder as I walked off. A short time later, I was waiting for him, standing at the chapel site holding a Bible and an American flag. Some of us were talking when I saw Ted coming our way.

"You can tell us good-bye, but don't rub it in," Ralph said as Ted walked up.

"Don't rush me off. I've got one more hour," Ted said as I showed him the jar with the Bible and flag inside it.

"So this is why you wanted me to come over?" Ted said with a cheerful smile.

"Yeah. Someday the chapel will be finished and we wanted you to seal the Bible and the flag in the cornerstone before you leave."

"Are we going to enclose our names?" Butch asked.

"I don't care about my name being left. That's not the reason we're building it." Shane replied.

"That's the way I feel too," Gary responded.

"The same for me. I don't care that my name be left either," Ted replied.

"And that goes for me too."

"I was just wondering, not that I really cared for my name to be left," Butch remarked.

I took the jar and tightened the lid and then asked Ted to place it in the stone. Then I watched him holding the jar as he looked toward the heavens with an expression I hadn't seen before. All was quiet with the passing moments as I was sure he was talking with God. Then quietly and very solemnly he turned to the stone and carefully placed the jar within. Then with the Bible and the American flag having been placed, I opened my Bible to the book of Psalms and read:

Make a joyful noise unto the Lord, all ye lands. Serve the Lord with gladness; come before His presence with singing. Know ye that the Lord, He is God; it is He that hath made us, and not we ourselves; we are His people and the sheep of His pasture. Enter into His gates with thanksgiving and into His courts with praise; be thankful unto Him and bless His name. For the Lord is good, His mercy is everlasting; and His truth endureth to all generations.

I closed the Bible and looked over at Ted. I knew the hour would soon be gone and his presence would become memories. The cement was mixed and very shortly the Bible and flag were sealed. A solemn mood prevailed. Ted had at most a few minutes left. I turned to him and asked him to lead us in a word of prayer. With heads bowed, his voice sounded:

Dear God, We thank you for this mountain. What you have allowed it to mean in each of our lives. Thank you for the love you've given, letting us have a closeness, one for the other. Now, God, as I depart, I pray for your blessings on all mankind and especially upon my fellow men as they continue to move forward, even in times when it seems impossible to build a place of worship on this mountain. Amen.

Ted, being one of the first who worked so hard on the chapel, was about to leave. He was talking with Shane and then he turned to me.

"Young'un, you remember the first nights back in the club, back when we first met?"

"Yeah, that's been some time ago, Ted, but I remember."

"You remember me riding you about the chapel? I didn't really mean anything by it."

"You were only joking us, Ted."

"Yeah, I was only joking you. Nothing more. Keep your guard up and keep the chapel going. Someday it'll be here."

"Thanks, Ted."

I listened to him calling Gimp as he walked off.

"We're going to miss him," Gary said as we watched him in the distance reaching down and rubbing Gimp's fur.

The noise from the engine sounded and we stood

watching him waving his hand as the truck moved down the mountain.

"The way Ted was drinking, even if the chapel is never finished it's done a lot of good," Shane remarked.

I listened to Shane's remark, hearing the echoing of the words, even if it's never finished. Then with a quick glance at the cornerstone, knowing that the Bible and flag were sealed, I was more determined than ever. We worked on through the day and then when night came I walked back to the chapel site. There I stood alone in the presence of God. Having thoughts of Ted, I walked over and sat down beside the cornerstone.

. . . .

In the days ahead, there was coldness and little daylight left in the evenings. It was Saturday morning, colder than any of the previous days. I left the mess hall on my way to meet Sergeant Rollins. As the whipping wind was penetrating my clothing, I dreaded the day ahead. At the top of the knoll I looked downward. I couldn't see anyone. At a further distance, I viewed the rippling of the waves. Thinking that Sergeant Rollins would be on pretty soon, I sat down and was meditating.

Dad, it was your words when you said, "The world is big and you're facing it, Son." You went on to say, "Love as we have loved one another." I know, Pop, how much you want me to come home, that you and Mom are happy in your thoughts, knowing that before long I'll be home. But I know the things you and Mom have taught me. It's not easy, Pop, just a bunch of lonely G.I.'s out on a mountain. I realize the world is big and the love that I've come to know, I want to give of it. We've got the chapel started but that's all. I feel the hurt from time to time, especially so as I see others leave. But I can't leave. You always said when you start

———◢———

146

*something that's good, try to finish it. And the chapel,
I told the major he'd be proud of it if he'd grant us
permission. But that doesn't matter, not really. But what
does matter is God's love as we partake of it in moving
through this life. So, Pop, the hurt is ours, but the good
is ours, too, as we share in the love that we've had with
one another.*

"Boyte!" the name sounded as it startled me.

"Yes, Sir," I responded, quickly standing to my feet.

"You dressed warm enough?"

"Yes, Sir. I think so."

"You're going to need a mattock and shovel. Haven't
you fellows got some?"

"Yes, Sir, some that we borrowed."

"You go get them and start digging here. You understand?"

"Yes, Sir, I understand."

"No bugging out. I'll be back to check on you."

"What about chow? Be okay if I stop long enough to
eat?"

"You better go on and get the shovel and mattock. We'll
take care of eating later."

"Yes, Sir."

"Boyte!" The voice sounded again as I walked off at a
distance.

"Yes, Sir."

"About chow."

"Yes, Sir."

"You can take off long enough to eat, but that's all."

"Thank you, Sergeant."

I turned and walked on to the chapel site. It was cold
and no one else was around. Grasping the shovel and mattock in my hand, I paused, staring at the cornerstone. "Ted,
it's not easy but we're not going to give up." Then I turned
and walked back to the knoll. Bracing myself for the day's

work ahead, I stiffened to the task. Lifting the mattock into the air, with a downward thrust it fell.

I kept feeling the roughness of the vibrations, hearing the shrillness from the clanging of the rocks. On through the long day I worked. Finally it was late in the evening and I was feeling tired. I stopped for a moment and sat down. There was no one in sight, only the flight of a bird as I pulled the harmonica from my pocket and started blowing. I was beginning to feel relaxed when Gimp nudged against my side. "Gimpy, old boy," I said, placing my arm around him. "It's you and me and it's going to be us for a long time." Suddenly, when Gimp lifted his head I turned. Off at a distance I could see Sergeant Rollins. Quickly I got to my feet and moments later Sergeant Rollins walked up. I was expecting to hear the sharpness of his voice. I waited. He didn't say anything. Finally he reached down and picked up a rock and then spoke.

"It was rough digging, wasn't it?" he said.

"Yes, Sir."

"And you did all this?"

"Yes, Sir, But it's taken all day."

"The foundation for the chapel, were the rocks this bad?"

"Yes, Sir."

"You fellows are really serious about building the chapel, aren't you?"

"Yes, Sir. It's going to take a long time, but someday it'll be finished."

"You know Sergeant Dooley, don't you?"

"Yes, Sir."

"About the lumber. You fellows did take it, didn't you?"

Pausing for a moment, I was frightened by the question. I didn't know what to say. But the tone of voice, the softness of the spoken words, there was only one way I could respond. "Yes, Sir, we did. We knew that it wasn't right. But we didn't have enough money, that was our problem. We thought we'd borrow the lumber and then return it. That way we could get something going."

"I see," Sergeant Rollins responded as he looked at the rock in his hand.

"It is rough going, isn't it?"

"Yes, Sir, it is."

"And you all do plan to return the lumber?"

"That's right. Otherwise we'd never have taken it."

I started to lift the mattock into the air again.

"There's no need to do any more. You've done enough. Let's go in."

With the mattock lowered and the day's work completed, I reached over and patted Gimp on the head.

. . . .

Through the passing of several days the weather conditions became better, and finally the long struggle to build the foundation was over.

Chapter 12

—◆—

Extending my time and watching the others leave wasn't easy. Yet being led by God to complete what we started, I stayed on. More than seven months passed since Ted and many of the others left. I stood with Gimp at my side viewing the completed days work. Placed in the front wall of the chapel above the vestibule was a cross we were putting in. When completed it would be lit at night, having dimensions of nine feet high, six feet wide, and a width of eighteen inches for the glass. I turned and looked out across the sea and for the first time I thought about the chapel facing Russia. Just maybe someday their people would have the freedom of worship, I thought. Then I walked over and sat down next to the cornerstone, having thoughts of Ted, Tom, Shane, Gary, and all the others. They worked so hard and we became so close.

Once the foundation was completed and word began to spread about the chapel, funds contributed by other soldiers began to trickle in from other units in Turkey, spreading on into Europe. Sergeant Dooley was gone and Sergeant Rollins, prior to leaving, became a strong supporter. Hoping that someday the chapel would be completed, he un-

—◆—

dertook efforts with the noncommissioned officers to get a continued fundraising project underway. The walls were nearing completion and the reality of the many dreams hoped for were nearer. Yet the struggles continued. Often from payday to payday, we would have to stop work and wait until more funds could be obtained. Ralph remained in the hut with me and continued to work on the chapel. The number of G.I.'s working on the chapel continued to increase. Like Ted and all the others said, "When we are gone, others will come and take our place."

When the new Major came in, he began to come over and talk with us about the chapel. One day he came by and was looking when he asked me to come by his office. I was somewhat nervous, not knowing what to expect when I went in, but he quickly put me at ease, asking that I have a cup of coffee with him. As we continued in conversation, he wanted to know about the early history of the chapel. I told him we got the approval from Major Brown to put up a temporary structure, a place where we could assemble and study the Bible, and when the chaplain did come in it would provide a place for worship. I went on to tell him that with the threat from the Soviet Union and the likelihood Sinop would become a large base, we were building the chapel so that it could be permanent and serve God, reaching out to mankind. Toward the completion of our conversation, he surprised me. In order that we might possibly have the chapel ready for Christmas, the two brick layers, Vic Theiman from California and John Brantly from Alabama, and I were relieved of all military duty, giving us full assignment to the chapel. Being relieved of all regular duty, we were able to get more done. Still, with the shortage of money, the lack of good tools to work with and only having the trucks in off duty hours, our work continued at a slow pace.

Much time was spent in trying to get good quality brick, usually at a distance of twenty-five to forty miles from the chapel. We learned that producing good quality brick was much different from that in the United States. Most often children would be in a dug pit working the mud up with their feet. From there the mud was placed in small wooden molds and then removed and stacked to be sun cured for three days. Then the bricks were placed in a crude kiln where they were fired by wood for several days. In selecting the bricks, we would take two at a time and hit them together, loading only those which gave a good ringing tone.

We were working on the chapel one Wednesday evening when Major Brown sent word for me. As I walked along toward his office it was a bright, sunshiny day with a few clouds in the sky, and there was a coolness of the breeze coming in off the sea. I stopped along the way and looked back, viewing the chapel that was finally rising upward into the air. John and some of the others were completing one of the side walls, while Vic was still laying brick around the cross. Being overwhelmed by the thought that God was seeing us through, I stood on a little longer. Then I reached down and stroked Gimp's fur and turned and headed on to the major's office. Before opening the door I tried to make sure that all the mud was removed from my boots. Then I removed my cap and stepped inside. Hank was doing some work at his desk, and with the door open to the major's office I could see Major Brown sitting in his chair. Just as I stepped forward I saw the major look up when Hank spoke.

"You got here quicker than I expected," he said.

"Charles said the Major wanted to see me."

"Yeah. I sent him over. How's the chapel coming along?"

"It's still going slow but we're working hard, trying to have it ready for Christmas."

"Sir, Boyte is here to see you."

"Send him in," I heard the major say.

I stood upright like a soldier should and stepped forward into the major's office. With a quick salute and the Major's return salute, I stood at ease.

"You wanted to see me, Sir?" I asked watching the major's serious expression.

"I've been looking at the cross in the chapel. It's pretty large, isn't it?"

"Yes, Sir. When it's finished, it'll be nine feet high, six feet wide, with a width of eighteen inches for the glass."

"You mentioned earlier you planned for it to be lit at night."

"We were hoping for that, Sir."

"You know the Turkish people are Muslim and we don't want to cause any problems."

"Yes, Sir. We understand."

"The reason I wanted you to come in, I wondered if we shouldn't check with the Governor about putting the cross in."

"We'll do whatever you say, Sir."

"It's just that the cross is so large, and then being lit up at night, I think it might be best."

"If you would like, Sir, we could leave the lights off."

"I thought about that but the cross stands out so much, I think it would be best for you to talk with the Governor."

"Yes, Sir. I'll take care of it."

"Have you talked with the Governor before?"

"No, Sir. I haven't."

"So as far as you know, no one has ever talked with the Governor about the chapel?"

"That's correct, Sir," I replied, having thoughts that Major Thomas gave his approval for a small temporary structure.

At first Major Brown didn't say anything. I could see from his expression he was concerned. "Building the chapel so large, it might have been good to have talked with the Governor first."

"Yes, Sir."

"Go ahead and talk with him. See what he says. You

can have Specialist Ziegler to set up the appointment and then have him to go with you."

"Yes, Sir. I'll talk with Specialist Ziegler and we'll take care of it." I left Major Brown's office with an empty feeling, wondering what the future of the chapel would be.

"Anything wrong?" Vic asked as I walked up.

"The news from the old man wasn't too good. You remember I told you we never got approval from the Turkish officials to build the chapel."

"So what did Major Brown have to say?"

"He first said because of the cross being lit up, he thought I ought to talk with the Governor. I told him we could leave the lights off and then he asked if anyone had ever talked with the Governor about building the chapel."

"So he wants you to talk with the Governor."

"Yeah, and I don't know what the outcome will be."

. . . .

Several days passed. I talked with Ziegler and the appointment was set up. I knew as we sat outside the Governor's office, waiting to see him, the future of the chapel depended on the next few minutes. Finally we were asked to go in. The door opened and we went in. Quickly, with the smiles and the hellos exchanged, I became more relaxed as Ziegler and I were invited to sit on the couch. In Turkey, hot tea was the drink. So it was no surprise when a few minutes later a small boy brought hot tea to us.

The Governor appeared to be a compassionate, friendly person, probably fifty years old. For the next several minutes we chatted back and forth, and when I told him I lived on the eastern coast of the United States near Fort Bragg there was a smile, as he acknowledged knowing something about Fort Bragg. Finally our chatting ended and we were ready to talk about the chapel. Ziegler was speaking in Turkish. When he mentioned the word chapel, the expression on the Governor's face showed no surprise. No doubt with a small Turkish military unit next to ours he had been up and possibly noticed the chapel.

"You're Christians and we're Muslims," he said with a smile looking over at me.

"*Evet*," I replied returning the smile, letting him know that I understood. With all the friendliness and the way he was responding, I was somewhat more relaxed. I knew very shortly we would have our answer.

"About the chapel, Governor, we wanted to find out if it would be okay to put a cross in the front wall?"

I watched the Governor as Ziegler interpreted what I said.

"The cross. That represents Jesus, doesn't it?" he said, responding with a serious expression.

"Yes, Sir. It does."

"You know," he said, and then paused for a moment before continuing to speak. "We're devout Muslims but I suppose for everyone it's important to worship God. You said the cross is in front of the chapel?"

"Yes, Sir. It is."

"And the chapel is facing toward Russia, isn't it?"

"Yes, Sir. It is."

"You know their leaders try to say there is no God."

"That's right, Sir. They just don't understand."

"And you wanted to know if it would be okay to put the cross in."

"Yes, Sir. But we don't want to cause any problems."

"Problems?" the Governor responded. "You know our problems are across the pond." Then with a smile he continued to speak. "We might ought to keep the cross in. Maybe it will help our friends across the pond."

Leaving the Governor's office, I was elated. I knew that God was guiding the building of the chapel. We acknowledged in the very beginning that only through Him could all the obstacles be overcome. I reported back to the Major and gave him the good news.

. . . .

Several days later, Ralph and I got up on Sunday morning. We ate chow and then with Gimp, we walked on toward the chapel. It was a pretty day and like so often, God's presence could be felt. There was the movement of a few clouds, one shaped like a whale and another like a mountain. Above the rippling waves of the sea a few birds were gliding through the flowing breeze of the air. It was just that kind of day, a special time to stop everything and spend it with God.

Surrounded only by the walls with no rooftop, there were eighteen of us in our Bible study. That didn't include Gimp, who was always our special visitor. We didn't have song books but we always sang the praises of God. Even Gimp joined in. It never failed. When we started singing, Gimp always started howling.

Later in the day I went by the club and from there Gimp and I headed down the mountainside. As I walked along, carrying a little food, I knew the boys would be waiting, waiting like they always did for Tom. Our closeness had grown for more than sixteen months. Almost every Sunday afternoon I spent some time with them. In all of our efforts to build the chapel, Taner was with us whenever possible, doing all that he could to help. Often times we left little Mehmet standing beside the road, waving to us as we drove off. Taking my time as I walked along, I took my harmonica out and started blowing it. Soon I stopped and listened to the lonesome sound of a ship's horn. Then, knowing that the boys should soon be coming into sight, I turned and started walking on. As I continued to walk further, I began to realize they were nowhere around. Finally I sat down. Soon Gimp walked over and nudged up against my side.

It had been more than an hour and still they hadn't come. Just as I was getting ready to leave, Gimp took off running down the mountain. At first I couldn't see anybody. Then at a distance I could see the movement of a child coming toward me. It was Taner. Suddenly I could sense something was wrong. With the tears falling and his arms extended, I didn't say anything. I just reached out and for the next several minutes held him in my arms. Finally he spoke.

"My brother can't walk."

"But last week he came."

"Not now. He can't walk. He want you to come."

"You're Turkish and I'm American. Are you sure it's okay?"

"It's okay. Come with me."

"But what about your mama? Are you sure it's okay?"

"Mama said for you to come."

Taner took hold of my hand. I wanted to go with him, but I didn't know what to do. We were always instructed not to do anything that could cause problems. Only once had I been in a Turkish home and there we were invited in for a meal. I knew it was risky, but soon we were on our way. We walked for approximately ten minutes and then, finally, we reached the house. Much like the house I was in before, there was an animal stall downstairs. Soon, with our shoes removed, I was somewhat surprised when Taner told me to wait. Then I watched his rapid movement going up the stairs. Very quickly he opened a door and almost immediately a Turkish woman, wearing a veil, came out and descended the stairs. She turned her head as she passed by. Never once did she look in my direction.

Taner was behind her. At first he took hold of my hand and then he turned it loose. He waited until his mother was out of sight. "My mama," he said and then he placed his hand on Gimp. "Come on Gimp," he said, trying to get him started up the stairs. I was watching Gimp when suddenly I realized what might be going on.

"No, Taner. Your mother might not want Gimp in the house."

"My mama not like, but my brother wants to see Gimp."

"I know. But we can't, not when I'm here."

"But Mehmet asked me to see Gimp."

"I understand, but we can't," I replied. Then for a moment all was quite. With nothing being said, I could see the hurt on Taner's face. Finally he spoke.

"When you not here, Gimp never comes."

"But some way we will get Gimp to come."

"No. When you not here, my mama is here. She won't let Gimp in."

I placed my arm around Taner and we started up the stairs. "You must understand. When I'm here we can't let Gimp in." Soon we were standing in the doorway. I looked across the room. Little Mehmet was looking at me as I moved toward his bed.

"Em," he said as he extended his hand with a little smile appearing. I didn't say anything as I handed him the little bag of goodies and then I took hold of his hand. Soon we were talking, almost laughing at times. I kept watching the movement of his legs under the cover, hoping that I might know more. Finally, some two hours later when Mehmet realized I was about to leave, the talking stopped. He held my hand firmly, like he didn't want to turn loose.

"Mehmet, I've got to go," I said.

"Gimp?" he asked.

"Gimp is outside but we can't bring him in." He said nothing more, only showing the feeling of hurt as he turned my hand loose. I wanted to reach back and take hold of his hand but I knew I couldn't. I just stood on and looked at him. There was an aging look in his hollowed eyes. Yet there was a youthfulness in his caring look, like he should be out on the mountainside with his hair tousling in the wind. Finally, with a pain of hurt, knowing something was bad wrong, I reached over and gently squeezed his hand and

---

said good-bye as I turned to leave. Going back up the mountain, along the way where the boys usually played didn't seem the same. It was night and the moon was shining. I stopped and took time to look up into the heavens. Then I bowed my head and prayed, asking God to touch the life of little Mehmet, that he might be healed. With my prayer finished, I stood looking into the darkness beyond, hearing only the crashing of the waves coming inland. Then as I thought about the vastness of the sea and the greatness of the universe I was overwhelmed by the thought of the Master of it all. A few minutes later I pulled the harmonica from my pocket and started blowing. Finally, knowing the hour was late Gimp and I headed in.

. . . .

For the next four weeks our progress on the chapel continued. The cross and the walls were completed. We were cutting the rafters and building the structured beams, making preparation to put the roof on. On each of the previous Sundays I spent the afternoons with Mehmet. His condition was worsening and I knew it wouldn't be long. It was again Sunday afternoon and I was on my way down. Throughout the week I remembered Mehmet's last look and what he had said as I was leaving. He held my hand firmly and asked about Gimp. I told him Gimp was outside waiting for him. Then he surprised me when he mentioned Tom's name and handed me the little picture of Gimp that Tom gave him. Tom and Gimp love you, I said as I reached over and hugged his neck. Then he said something I didn't understand.

"I love you," Taner repeated.

"I love you," I replied feeling his love penetrating within me.

"You come back," he said.

"I will. I'll bring you something special."

Earlier in the week I took a picture of Gimp and had it developed into a large picture. Then I spent a lot of time working with an old frame, trying to make the gift something special, something that he would always remember. Gimp was at my side and we were moving along quickly. With a feeling of joy, I knew that when I handed him the bag and watched him pull the picture out, I would see that little smile again. "We're almost there, Gimpy," I said, reaching down, stroking his fur. "You know something, old fellow, I told you a long time ago, you give life to all of us. Mehmet needs you. He's been wanting to see you. You see this, old fellow," I said pulling the picture out. "This is you, just for Mehmet." Finally in the distance I could see the house. I was getting nearer. It looked like the old seaman, Hasan, standing with Taner in the yard. Suddenly when Gimp took off in a trot, I picked up the pace, running along behind him. Then all at once an empty feeling came. Mehmet was gone. I could see it in Taner's eyes as the tears were flowing. I reached out and embraced him in my arms and then finally several minutes later Taner reached down and began to stroke Gimp's fur.

"He wanted to see you, Gimpy," Taner said.

A few tears began to come as I held the picture firmly in the bag. Soon Taner, Gimp, and I were standing at the grave. Watching Taner cry, I reached out again and embraced him in my arms.

Finally, knowing that it was all over with, I reached down and rubbed Gimp's fur. "He loved you Gimpy," I said as I pulled the picture out and placed it on the grave. Then I reached out and took hold of Taner's hand and we turned and walked off. A short time later Taner, Gimp and I were back at our usual place on the mountainside but it wasn't the same. Taner reached down and picked up the ball that Mehmet had played with so many times and when he started crying I placed my arm around his shoulder. I wanted to tell him about Jesus but I never said anything. I knew he was a

Muslim and I was an American soldier under strict guide-lines. As we sat on the ground and I looked across the far distance of the sea, I felt a loneliness for time gone by. Like I wanted to again experience Gimp, Tom and the boys in their joyful play. Finally the time came. It was twilight and there was a redness in the sky. I was blowing the harmonica, watching Taner go down the mountain. When he turned and waved, I knew the love God had given us would always be part of me.

Chapter 13

---■---

It was November 25, 1958. Ralph and I were standing at mail call, waiting for the shutters to open. At a distance I could see the chapel with the partially completed steeple rising upward into the air.

"This is my last mail call," Ralph said.

"I know. I was just thinking about the first night you came in."

"I just can't wait," Ralph said as he pulled his wallet out and looked at the pictures of his wife and son.

I was happy for him, knowing that he and his family would be together at Christmas. Still, I hated to see him leave. For twelve months we'd been together. We slept in bunks side by side, sharing the good times and the bad times. Finally the shutters opened and I watched Ralph reach for his letter and then shortly my name was called. I opened my letter and started reading.

> *Dear Son,*
> *We're looking forward to your coming home. We miss you so much and we want you to be careful. Joe continues to do well at Elon College. You know that he*

---■---

has the G.I. Bill. John was in last weekend and Sylvia is finally enrolled in a school where she can work her way through nurse's training.

Last Sunday we all got up and ate breakfast and then we went to church. When I showed the pictures of the chapel, they got all excited. They wanted me to ask you about hymn books. I think they'd like to send them if it's okay. You just let me know. Your dad is proud of the chapel. Just the other day he was talking with Davis. You would have been proud to see that big smile when he pulled the picture out of his bib pocket and showed it.

At first when we learned you wouldn't be coming home, it hurt us but we understood. Your dad continues to have difficulty with his walking. You know how it was when you left. Now that your time is becoming less, I occasionally see him standing out in the field. Just this morning he was talking about the pines beginning to grow. He's hoping that when you get home, you all will be able to get a tractor and do some farming. You know how you and your dad always talked about farming. It means so much to him . . .

With a feeling of closeness to home, I finished reading the letter and then went back to my hut. There I sat looking at the replica of the chapel, thinking of all the times gone by. Finally I reached over and picked up my Bible and started reading. Being comforted by the reading of God's word, I left the hut and walked to the chapel. As I stood and looked at its beauty and thought about the many nights we struggled, it all seemed like a dream.

. . . .

The next four weeks passed quickly. It was Tuesday evening, December 23. I was standing in front of the chapel admiring the star placed on the steeple. Even though work remained to be done, we were all excited at the thought of Christmas worship in the chapel. Gimp and I walked over and sat down next to the cornerstone. Soon his head was resting in my lap and I was stroking his fur, having thoughts of Ted, Tom, Shane, and all the others. There were so many dreams and hopes and now so much to remember. If only I could share the beauty of the chapel with them, I thought.

Suddenly, when Gimp raised his head, I looked up. It was Major Brown and another officer. Quickly I stood up and gave a salute. With a return salute, Major Brown smiled and shook my hand.

"I've got some good news for you," he said. "I would like for you to meet Chaplin Paznonskas. He has been assigned full time to us."

The next hour was a happy occasion as we toured the chapel and I told them about the many experiences we'd been through and how we took the wrecked trucks and cut the chassis up to get our steel. Toward the conclusion of our conversation Chaplain Paznonskas told me the story of the chapel was known widely by a lot of people and that soon we would be receiving a grant from the Chief of Army Chaplains in Arlington, Virginia. He also told me an organ was being shipped in, and then just as they were about to leave, Major Brown said, "I've got some more good news for you."

"More good news? What is it, Sir?"

"The chapel is our first permanent building. The inspection team that came in from Germany went back and redesigned the whole base to be built around the chapel. I thought you'd like to hear that."

"Yes, Sir. That's really good news and we're glad to have Chaplain Paznonskas with us too."

After the major and the chaplain left, I went back into the chapel and spent time with God, kneeling at the altar. Although the finished flooring was still to be completed, it was a joyous occasion knowing that the next day on Christmas Eve the true meaning of Christmas would be observed by worship in the chapel.

. . . .

Finally the time came. As I took my seat and looked around, I could feel the presence of God, knowing that He was pleased with the occasion. Just as we started to sing, Gimp came forward and started to howl. Then as the service continued, knowing that the chapel was permanent and the chaplain was full time, it was a marvelous feeling to know that when we place God first, His work will be done through us.

. . . .

Soon Christmas was over, and two months later I stood in reverence before God, giving thanks for the beautiful chapel that stood completed high on the mountain. There were no words that could express the feeling—only the love that existed between God and me. As my time was drawing nigh each moment seemed to be more precious. In one of my last conversations with the chaplain, I told him about our decision to leave no names in the cornerstone. Finally there were only a few minutes left and I would be boarding the truck. I had been on the mountain for twenty-six months, and during that time I saw many new faces come and old faces leave. With Gimp at my side I went in the chapel for the last time and knelt at the altar.

Finally the time was at hand. I loaded my baggage and said good-bye. Then I reached down and took a little time with Gimp. Soon I was on the truck and we were headed down the mountain. I watched Gimp trailing along behind, trying desperately to keep up, but with our speed continuing to increase I knew it couldn't be long. "Gimpy, old boy," I said to myself. "It's over. You go on back." Then I turned and looked out across the mountain where Tom, the boys and I always met. As the truck moved on into the distance, taking us further away, I turned and looked at the chapel for the last time. Then I looked upward into the sky. Seeing the brightness of the moon shining brighter than ever before, *Dad*, I said to myself, *it's finished. I'm coming home.*

Then I looked beyond the brightness of the moon into the depth of the heavens, and with joy I gave thanks to God, knowing that I was traveling homeward.

Epilogue

---◆---

No record with names was left with the chapel. It was only through inquiry of a student of mine that twenty-one years later I learned that housed in the vestibule of the chapel is a bronze plaque with the inscription below.

DEDICATION

This chapel is a monument to the moving spirit and effort of the American soldiers stationed here in 1957 and 1958. At the suggestion of a visiting chaplain and with the blessing of the commanding officer, the men began the project of financing and building a chapel.

Funds were obtained through voluntary contributions from the men, donations from sister units in Europe and a grant from the Chief of Army Chaplains. Under soldier planning and supervision, after-duty volunteers dug foundation, poured cement and began to raise the brick walls. The work halted only when money and materials were exhausted.

After almost two years of building, the first religious services were held in the chapel on Christmas Eve 1958. This house of God stands as a symbol of the zeal and dedication of the men who gave their time and ability to the glory and honor of God and our country.

---◆---

*Photos from the
U.S. Military Base
and Chapel site, Sinop, Turkey.*

Mail call—first building on the right.

Christmas Eve, 1958. First worship service in the chapel.

The Chapel, March 1959

The finished Chapel (see cover).

About the Author

James (Jim) Boyte was born and raised in rural North Carolina. After graduating from high school and being unable to find permanent work, he joined the army. Soon after completing basic training, he volunteered for duty in the remote area of Sinop, Turkey. While stationed there, Jim was instrumental in the construction of a chapel which eventually inspired him to write *Look Homeward*. After leaving the military, he worked his way through school to earn the Ph.D. in Mathematics.

Jim and his family live on the family farm near Carthage where he grew up and now farms and is a professor of mathematics. He and his wife, Jan, are the proud parents of five children: Jim, Jr., Timothy, Stephen, Jonathan and Tammy.